Growing Up in

Rat City

and Beyond

Alexander G. Sasonoff

authorHOUSE®

AuthorHouse™
1663 Liberty Drive, Suite 200
Bloomington, IN 47403
www.authorhouse.com
Phone: 1-800-839-8640

First published by AuthorHouse 9/24/2008

ISBN: 978-1-4343-8903-9 (sc)

Library of Congress Control Number: 2008905386

Printed in the United States of America
Bloomington, Indiana

This book is printed on acid-free paper.

Acknowledgements

A number of people helped me in the preparation of this book. I want to thank all of them for their suggestions and contributions.

My gratitude goes to my brother Leon Sasonoff who read the manuscript several times, correcting grammar and helping with the Russian translations. Thanks to Scott Robinson for typing the first writings of the manuscript and to Brooke Bearg who patiently typed and retyped the manuscript many times as it progressed. Thanks to one of my earliest childhood friends, Dr. Robert W. Clarke, retired professor of English literature, who read portions of the manuscript and provided valuable thoughts. Another friend from Rat City, Dr. Virginia Frost, read portions of the manuscript and provided assistance. My friend Delbert Wickline who also grew up in Rat City provided me with memories that we had shared together. Thanks to Gary Coy for lending me his photos of the old White Center Theater.

Dedication

This book is dedicated to my daughters Mauria and Alixine with love.

Part I • The Move to Rat City

The Move

As I sat in the front seat of the moving van clutching my cat, Reezhik, I had mixed feelings about moving to the house my parents had purchased near White Center. I was leaving all of my friends at F.A. McDonald Grade School as well as the other kids in my neighborhood. It was 1936 and the Boeing Aircraft Company was hiring workers. My Dad landed a job there.

The drums of war were starting their death rattle in Europe and the U.S. government ordered the construction of thirteen B17 bombers. These same thirteen bombers were flying into Hawaii when the Japanese attacked Pearl Harbor. It was a typical gray overcast day in Seattle. We were moving during a mid-school term so I would have to start all over again with new friends. Many good memories were being left behind. We lived across the street from lower Woodland Park. There were many picnics in the park and on the shores of Greenlake. Visits to the zoo will always be with me.

The driver of the moving van hated cats and threatened, if the cat got loose, he was going to throw him out the window. I tightened my grip on Reezhik. He made me sit as far from him as possible so I was squeezed up against the door panel with my brother, my Dad sat in the middle. I could not convey the threat to my cat but the cat must have sensed the hatred and did not move. Our dog, Spot, had already been safely transported to his new home.

It took about two hours in the lumbering moving van to get from Green Lake to our destination. We arrived without incident. The house was located on a double lot so there was plenty of space to play. Fruit trees abounded, there were apple, cherry, pear, plum and peach throughout the yard.

The oldest portion of the house used to be an office for a logging company that had cut all the timber in the area years before. It rested on a log foundation with the rest of the house added later. The newer portion had a very strange concrete foundation. I believe the basement was dug out after the house was constructed. The concrete was stepped and appeared to be about two feet thick. There were no sewers in the area and all of the streets were gravel. The sewage system was a simple cesspool that we all were warned to stay away from for fear of the wood planks collapsing.

Years later this area was sewered and after that came paved streets and sidewalks. My brother, Leon and I shared one bedroom while my two sisters, Vera and Ireda shared another. Later, we refurbished the attic creating two more bedrooms, so eventually each of us had our own room.

The house had only one bathroom. The water was heated by a coil of pipes in the wood burning furnace and kitchen stove. In the summertime there was never enough hot water generated by the kitchen stove. It was too warm to fire up the big furnace. Kettles of water were heated atop the kitchen stove to supplant the weekend baths. To save hot water, my brother and I used the same bath water.

This became a greater problem when our cousin moved in with us after being freed from a Japanese prison camp after the war. My Dad used to call me into the bathroom to wash his back. He sat in the tub while shaving. On one such occasion I asked him why he did not have any gray hair. I had noticed everyone getting on in years had gray hair. He answered me in Russian, *"Ya vsegda moyu golavoo s holodnoi vodom."* Translated, "I always wash my head with cold water."

As the years passed and when I was in my twenties, washing my hair with cold water, I burst out laughing at the realization that he was telling me to keep a cool head. In that old house we finally had an electric hot water tank installed and there was much rejoicing.

In 1936 most of the country was still struggling from the years of Depression. Our spacious yard provided a place to plant a garden and raise some of our own vegetables. A chicken house was added and later, a place for ducks. We also raised turkeys. My parents were unaware that turkeys had to be kept away from other feathered fowl. Chickens carried a disease called blackhead. It does not affect chickens but it is fatal to turkeys. The turkeys, chickens and ducks shared the same yard area. It was sad to have them killed after they had grown to be about ten or twelve pounds; however one turkey did make it to Thanksgiving, weighing in at nearly 40 pounds. This large survivor was very protective of his territory and he would chase dogs and strangers. His head would turn bright red, his wings would spread out and he would lower his head and charge. The ducks did just fine in the rainy weather and would fly around the neighborhood, always returning to their pens in the evening.

One day a duck turned up missing. We looked all over the neighborhood. No luck, no duck. On a few occasions, I had seen a duck sitting on a neighbor's chimney, so I told my dad. He reluctantly got out a ladder and climbed onto the roof. In the chimney, about as far down as he could reach was the duck. The rescue was successful.

With the ducks and the chickens there was always meat on the table along with eggs. The yard was planted with a variety of vegetables and berries as well. We had raspberries, loganberries, boysenberries, gooseberries and strawberries. When all of these ripened mother would cook and can many jars of jams and jellies, not to mention peas, beans and beets.

Even though we had a dining room, meals were always served at the kitchen table. The dining room was reserved for special occasions. The living room was always kept ready for the unexpected guest as was customary for homes in the old world. We were not allowed to play there. At the dinner table if someone accidentally dropped a morsel of food on the floor, my Dad would sharply exclaim in Russian, *"Povalyai, povalyai, boodet v kooskneiya."* Translated, he was saying, "Roll it around, roll it around, it will taste better."

My parents did not know very much about White Center or the Puget Sound region. They emigrated to the U.S. from Russia by way of China. My dad arrived in 1923, but mother had to wait for the next quota and didn't arrive until 1928. My brother Leon was born in 1929, myself in 1930 and sister Vera in 1932 with sister Ireda being born in 1936. Sadly, two other sisters, Diane and Virginia died as infants in China—one of scarlet fever and the other of diphtheria, both treatable diseases today.

We had no automobile so we always made our way by streetcar or bus and more often than not we walked to Highland Park Grade School which was only three blocks away or on Saturdays as far as White Center for feed for the chickens or hardware items.

Short Pants

After moving to White Center we had to be registered in school. It was mid-term and classes were already in session. All the boxes of clothing had not yet been unpacked. My mother was scrambling through the boxes trying to find pants that my brother and I could wear. The only thing she could find was our short pants and she said we would have to wear them. All the other boys wore long pants and only sissies wore short pants. We pleaded with her not to make us wear those sissy pants, to no avail. With all the classes in session and after registering, we were taken to each classroom to be introduced. I could hear the kids snickering.

It was particularly humiliating to stand in the front of the class in short pants. During recess and at lunchtime Leon and I received even more disparaging remarks. We lived through that first day, but it was some time before we were accepted as equals.

During recess periods there were all sorts of games to be played. The most popular at that time was marbles. A circle would be drawn in the dirt and each player would put into the circle a specified number of marbles. Another line would be scratched into the earth and each player would peg his shooter to see who would be first. The player closest to the line would go first. Being first was a great advantage as you had the greatest number of marbles to shoot at. Rules were shouted out as different things happened during the game. If your shooter didn't get out of the ring you could shout "changees" and replace your shooter with a giant marble or a pea-sized marble so the next shooter could not knock your shooter out of the ring. If he did it would cost you extra marbles. There was a term "no raisees" which meant that you couldn't shoot by raising your shooting hand on top of your second hand, which acted as a support providing additional elevation to shoot over the top of the other marbles. It was such a simple game but it kept everyone, even some troublemakers, occupied and out of mischief.

Marbles were fun, but the pride of every young boy was to have a pocketknife. If you were lucky enough to have one it would be passed around for everyone to see so they could ooh and aah. Games were played throwing knives at vertical wood obstacles and a game called "mumbly peg" was played where you rolled an open knife off of various parts of your body to stick into the ground. As the game progresses, each task is more difficult. The loser has to pull a wooden peg from the earth with his teeth that has been driven into the ground by the winner. No one ever thought of stabbing or injuring fellow playmates and I think just about everybody yearned to own a pocketknife. Some of the kids would go into the woods next to the school and cut willow branches to fashion flutes. Woods and empty lots, swamps and ponds were to be found everywhere at the time and were great places for adventure and for cowboy and Indian battles.

The Teachers

Miss O'Brien was the English teacher at Highland Park Grade School. A spinster, (in those days women could not be married and teach), she was a small, frail stick of a woman with a hawkish face, her hair pulled back into a tight bun. Her nose was very sharp and bird-like, upon which rested round wire-framed glasses. Her mouth was small and her upper lip would scrunch up when she talked, giving her the appearance of being angry. In fact, there were many occasions when she was angry! If you disobeyed or did not study your lesson, her Irish temper would explode sending you to the corner in front of the class. I experienced the humiliation a number of times myself. Standing with

6

my face wedged into the corner, I thought my nose would begin to look like hers.

Another thing that she had a habit of doing was to suddenly fly down the aisle and start beating a hapless student on the back with clenched fists connected to her broomstick arms. My friend Donny Chase was a frequent recipient of those attacks. One day Miss O'Brien appeared with her arm in a large cast. We all thought, my god, if she lands on someone's back with that club, there would be serious damage. Fortunately, the broken arm sharply reduced the number of beatings. We started a rumor that she had broken her arm beating on Donny's back. One of Miss O'Brien's favorite sayings was, "I wish the tops of your heads were garbage can lids so I could just raise them and pour the knowledge in." I never did like that class and could not understand why one needed to know the difference between a noun and a verb.

Ms. O'Brien

For serious misbehaviors in or out of class, a visit to the principal's office was a given. Mr. Knutson was not very big, but he could really pack a wallop with the leather strap that hung on the wall behind his desk. To receive your punishment, you would be instructed to grab your ankles after which with a whop, the leather would fly. The embarrassment of it all was worse than the pain. In no time the whole school knew who got what. For the rest of the day the other kids would tease you for having had the experience. But such was the discipline of the time and I don't believe anyone suffered permanent damage for undergoing the ordeal.

Our music teacher, Miss Schetler, had a different method for discipline. She was probably in her early fifties and appeared to spend a great deal of time coiffing her hair and over-applying her makeup. She wore thick glasses along with her stern Germanic look. A misbehaving student would be sent to the music storage room and instructed to hold his hands out with the palms down. A thick ruler would come crashing down on the backs of those hands. I must say that this was quite painful, but the lesson was learned and again, no lasting damage to my ego.

Our reading and writing teacher was Miss Fickeisen. I never had any trouble in that class and enjoyed it. She was always encouraging students to read and I believe that is when I became interested in books. She would approach a student privately and tell them, "This book that I have in my hand just came into our library. Before anyone else reads it, I am giving you the first opportunity to read it. I know you like to read so I am making this offer to you first, but don't tell anyone that I favored you." With a touch like that how could anyone refuse? Later it was discovered that she was saying the same thing to all of the students. It was a clever ploy to get students to read.

Mr. Cable was our shop teacher. A tall man with black hair, his chin was so thick and dark with stubble that even when he shaved it looked as though he hadn't. With dark piercing eyes behind black-rimmed glasses he had a fierce appearance. This was an all-boys class and Mr. Cable would let his temper fly when disciplining the students. I think he was concerned with preventing injuries while we worked with various woodworking tools. Behind his blustery manner was a kind and understanding human being. If I had a question about a tool or some work I was doing, he would take a great deal of time explaining the tool or in describing how to use it.

The war was fully on by this time and a representative from the U.S. Navy came to our school and talked to Mr. Cable. The military needed scale model planes that could be used to teach Navy personnel about aircraft identification. It was a unique assignment and exciting as all of us had our favorite warplane. We were each given solid blocks of pine to carve into a model of our choice. The wing and tail assemblies were carved separately and glued to the body. The model was painted flat black to be used for silhouette identification. Upon completion the Navy gave each student a certificate of commendation.

Mr. Fields was our gymnasium teacher. He was very short and having been a tumbler and gymnast, was always directing our activities toward tumbling and working on the bars. At that time I was not well coordinated and had difficulty tumbling. Mr. Fields would sit on the bench and as we ran up to the mat to do our flips, he would lend a helping hand to complete the exercise.

Mr. Fields was also a tough disciplinarian. While playing soccer, a disagreement arose, and for some reason I was in the middle of it. The other kids were goading me into a fight with a boy named Patrick Gallagher. I wasn't even mad at him. The shouting was going on around the circle that the other boys had formed around us. "Hit him, hit him!" they shouted at me and they began pushing us around in the circle. I decided that I had better take a swing at Patrick, but as I did, I accidentally stepped on his foot. When I hit him, down he went.

Mr. Fields came out of the gym just in time to see me strike Patrick and knock him down. I was ordered into the storage room and told to grab my ankles. Mr. Fields used his bare hand to whack me a few times, and again, the embarrassment was worse than the pain. The nice part of all this was that Patrick and I became very good friends.

Miss Lorentzen was our art teacher and she allowed us free hand to draw whatever we wanted. I remember drawing army airplanes, as most of the other boys did. Mrs. Lorentzen was an artist and upon seeing my sister Vera, wanted to do an oil painting of her. Vera had very long hair that was put up in braids. This braided hair with a child's face made a very striking appearance for a portrait. The sitting was arranged with my parents' approval. It would be done at school on Saturdays. My mother said I would have to go along to protect my sister. I didn't mind as Mrs. Lorentzen gave me the run of the art room to do as I wished. This went on for a number of Saturdays until the portrait was completed. It is too bad we were not able to get a photo of the finished painting. I have often wondered what happened to that painting.

Two other teachers I remember are Miss Aiken, who taught geography, and Miss Houston who taught history. For some reason, there was nothing in these classes that inspired me. Listening to the teachers drone on about subjects I had no interest in drove me to draw doodles as I sat in the last row of seats. Some of these doodles were nasty and one day Miss Houston caught me. She called me into the hall and as she lectured me, all my energy vanished and I went limp. From then on I paid attention in class.

Discipline justly applied is not a bad thing. I deserved each reprimand received. Through discipline, the classroom was a very orderly place. You were not allowed to talk unless asked to speak. You were not allowed to chew gum. I remember looking under the desks and found them plastered with gobs of gum.

Miss Hader was our science teacher. She was probably the youngest of all our teachers. We would take classes on short field trips into the woods next to the school to collect leaves, frogs and their eggs that abounded in the many swamps located there. All these items were brought into class for further study. One funny incident that happened in this class is worth mentioning. The science class was our first period class where roll was taken to make sure all were present. Willie Haskins was a very shy kid and was easily embarrassed. At that time, Lindbergh, the world famous pilot was still looked upon as a hero. One item of clothing that was a favorite among the young boys was the leather Lindbergh flying helmet. All the boys envied those who had them. Willie came into the classroom wearing his Lindbergh hat. Protocol was that all outer garments, including hats, had to be stored in the lockers before entering the classroom. Willie was a tall gawky kid with long blond hair. Miss Hader told him to remove his hat, which he refused to do. Miss Hader went round and round with Willie and he still refused. Miss Hader was getting angry and threatened to send Willie to the principal. The situation was escalating and getting uncomfortable. Willie hung onto the straps of his helmet as Miss Hader tried forcibly to remove it. Finally Willie removed his hat to expose a head of butchered hair. His long locks of blond hair were gone, revealing stumps and clumps sticking out in all directions. His face reddened and he slumped into his seat. Miss Hader, feeling sorry for him, let him put his hat back on. Many of the families in this neighborhood did not have much money, so haircuts were done at home. Poor Willie was the victim of a disastrous home cut.

A Trip To White Center

White Center straddles the county line with the business district being both in Seattle and King County. It is a composite of various commercial establishments, surrounded by single-family housing occupied by blue-collar families. It received its name in 1918 with a coin toss between a Mr. White and a Mr. Green. Had the coin flipped over one more time, I might have grown up in Green Center.

At the age of six, eye level is about three feet six inches from the ground. This gives one a different perspective of the world. Walking about in

White Center, I could easily peer under the swinging tavern doors of which there were many. The raucous laughter and other sounds that emanated from within aroused my boyish curiosity. It seemed that every other store front was a tavern. The heavy smell of beer wafted out through those doors and filled the air. Whenever I smell beer today, memories of early White Center flood my mind's eye.

Many years later, while serving in the Army, I met a guy named Fred who had been in the merchant marine. We were both stationed at Fort Monmouth in New Jersey and while having a friendly conversation he asked where I was from. When I told him I hailed from White Center, he then surprised me with the following story: His ship had pulled into Seattle and he had asked his mates where was a fun place to go in the city. They told him to head for White Center. He hailed a cab and asked the cabbie where would be the best spot to have a drink. He was dropped off at the Glendale Tavern, an old well-established watering hole frequented by locals who often got into fights and did not cotton to strangers. One of them was an off-duty policeman that patrolled the area and tried to keep things somewhat orderly. The cop was about six feet six inches tall and his real name was Tommy Tucker. Of course it wasn't long before he was nicknamed Tiny. The owner of The Glendale was a very large, buxom woman named Ma Ritchie. (She tended bar there and many years later was to come into my life as a personal friend.) But, back to the story with Fred. He walks through the swinging doors and as soon as he is inside, someone punches him in the face. He is sent flying backwards and out into the street. He struggles to his feet and starts for the door again when, BAM! he is hit again and lands in the street again. At this point, Fred decided that he'd had enough, called for another cab and went back to the ship. That was what he remembered about White Center. I had no idea that I lived in such a famous place. In those days dislikes and disagreements were settled by your fists, not with guns as is the case all too often today.

Roxbury Street was the designated county line that separated White Center from the City of Seattle. The north half is in Seattle and the south half in King County. Roxbury runs east-west and was a graveled road from 16th Avenue to Olson Place, which leads me to the following story: Billy Campbell's dad had an old 1934 Studebaker which was a flat charcoal color. It was built like a tank. Billy's dad would let him use the car on occasion. A lot of us neighborhood kids would pile into it and go for joyrides. At this particular intersection, Billy took the corner too fast. The car slid sideways on the gravel and took out a row of mailboxes and just missed a power pole. The right front fender and the headlight were damaged. It was the last time Billy's dad let him use the car. It was fortunate that there were no injuries.

Many years ago, prize fighting in Seattle was severely limited by permits, licenses and other legalities, hence a boxing ring was constructed on the county side of Roxbury Street. Prizefights were held there attracting a rough and rowdy drinking and betting crowd. The ring was built by Hiram Green and later converted to a roller-skating rink still in operation today. There were many prizefighters from this working-class area. One of them, Al Hostak, held the middleweight championship of the world. After his retirement, Al tended bar for many years at the Epicure restaurant up the street from the Glendale Tavern. This establishment was there for many years and was well attended by locals. I remember fundraisers held there for Washington's Governor Rossellini.

Another fighter, Harry Kid Mathews, lived on the city side of White Center. The Kid went on from White Center to fight the famous Bostonian Heavy Weight Champion of the World, Rocky Marciano. Unfortunately, he was knocked out in the second round. Still Mathews career as a boxer was significant. He knocked out 43 opponents in 49 fights, fighting in three different weight divisions, including heavyweight. My former wife's family was well acquainted with Kid Matthews and we used to party at the Angle Lake Plunge. The Plunge was a place not far from White Center where one could bring his own liquor, pay a cover charge and dance to live band music. Mixers for drinks were purchased for a nominal fee.

Another one of my neighbors was a fighter named Jackie Moore. Jackie fought in the lightweight division and gained notoriety there. His dad was a retired prizefighter and used to teach neighborhood kids the fundamentals of boxing. Jackie's dad worked at the Frye packing plant in Seattle. He wielded a sledgehammer to put down beef cattle. It wasn't pleasant listening to stories about his work. It was the Frye packing plant that was damaged when one of the early B29 bombers crashed into it.

Back in the 1920s and 1930s, hard liquor was not available in taverns. It was introduced to White Center sometime later through private bottle clubs. Laws were later passed to allow cocktail lounges in restaurants. Sprinkled among the taverns were a number of commercial businesses. In this colorful mix were two drug stores—White Center Drug and Olberg's Thrifty Drugs, which had a soda fountain. Also in town were Bunge Lumber and Hardware, Dupre's Department Store, Coy's Center Theater, Neupert's Market, Kremen's 5 & 10 Cent Store, the skating rink, Busey's Drive In, the Dapas junkyard, Yarington's Funeral Home and the Feed & Seed store.

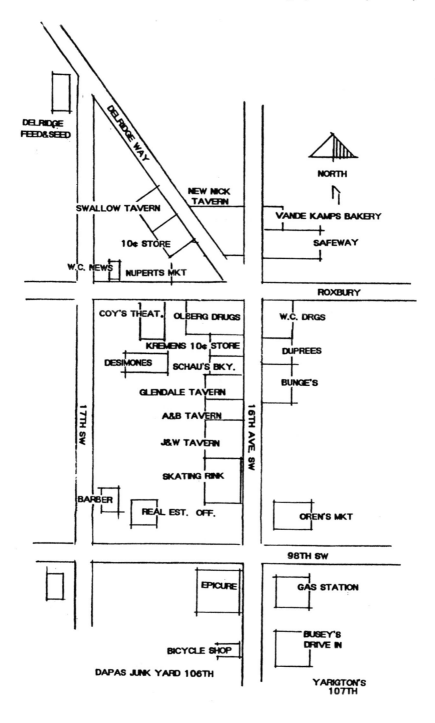

Bunge Lumber and Hardware was an interesting store Supplying everything save for groceries, service was always on a personal basis. The clerk, Elmer Matson would help you find whatever you needed. Years later as an architect, I designed a home for Elmer and his wife. In the store one could buy nuts, bolts, nails, screws, lumber, coal, firewood, creosote, all manner of cookery items, wooden mixing bowls, and hand juicers made of green glass and most importantly, fishing tackle—lures, spinners and all kinds of colorful flies. There were sleds, wagons, seeds and bulbs. On the walls hung rolls of screen material for repairing window and door screens. Bunge was the forerunner of the big box stores of today, and whenever my brother and I went into town with Dad for supplies we always stopped at Bunge's because there was always something there to peak a boy's interest. Mr. Bunge would give me a patronizing pat on the head and comment on how fast I was growing. He had a full head of hair that was white as snow and he would be sitting behind his desk wearing a fedora. In those days every man wore a hat. He lived to be 97 years of age and he came to work everyday right up to the very end. One year, I purchased a wooden mixing bowl for a Mother's Day gift. I inherited that bowl and use it quite often. On the bottom, written in pencil is the price. Now barely visible, one can still read 90 cents.

After our visit to the hardware store, Dad would always stop and have a glass of beer (5 cents at the time) at the Swallow Tavern. My brother and I waited patiently outside peering in through the windows at the noisy patrons and the sawdust floor.

Public transportation in White Center was not readily available, and if the bus wasn't standing at the bus stop, you could count on a half-hour's walk home. If you waited for a bus, you could be standing there for a long time. A street car used to run to White Center, but three years before we moved there it was taken out of service, sidetracked at 9ᵗʰ and S.W. Henderson St. It soon became an ideal place for kids to play. We all wanted to be the conductor, taking turns pretending to run the trolley.

Most of the streets were not paved in those days and during hot summers clouds of dust were raised by any moving vehicle. The dust descended on the residences and businesses leaving people, vegetation and homes in a fine layer of dust.

Highland Park Way was known as Boeing Hill. The original Red Barn, Boeing's first building where Mr. Boeing started making WWI fighters and later the Pan American Flying Boats, was located at the foot of the steep hill. Though that street was paved, it only had two lanes. The trolley car could not negotiate the steep grade so the road and tracks parted at the top of the hill at the intersection of Holden St. and Highland Park Way. At this point, the trolley tracks disappeared into the woods at a much shallower grade, and then came out of the woods at the bottom of the hill along West Marginal Way. From there the tracks followed the Duwamish River and then across Spokane St. into downtown Seattle. There were many earth slides due to rains that loosened the clay underlying most of Seattle. These occurred along the tracks in the wooded area so it was eventually abandoned, making for a wonderful access deep into the woods for kids to play.

One day as we walked the old rail bed we came across a large hole burrowed into the hillside. I was with my friends Earl and George Hannon and their dog, Rex. Rex dove into the burrow and in a few moments he came out dragging a wild rabbit. We had much difficulty trying to carry that rabbit home, with the yapping dog and the rabbit trying to bite us. Earl's Dad constructed a pen for the rabbit that did not like his new home and kept gnawing giant holes in the wood. We finally released him to the neighboring woods.

The Army Moves In

To protect the Boeing plant and airfield the military had moved in along the High Ridge areas surrounding the valley where the factories were located and also along 12th Avenue north of Holden Street in the area where South Seattle Community College is now. They installed tents and later many barracks and barrage balloons to trap incoming enemy aircraft. Early in the morning military personnel would also send up weather balloons. I was delivering *The Post-Intelligencer* at the time and some of the soldiers were my subscribers. When those soldiers were suddenly transferred out, of course I was the monetary loser. Still, it gave me a patriotic feeling to deliver the daily news to the camp. I was in the Boy Scouts at that time and one of the soldiers gave me a sleeping bag to use on scout outings. The zipper did not work very well, but I was thrilled to have it since there was never enough money for such a luxury item.

The four anti-aircraft guns placed next to our school had to be maintained. The officer in charge told our principal that the guns would be fired for practice periodically. Even though the ammunition was powder charges only, we were instructed to keep all the windows opened slightly so they would not be broken by the concussion. When this was announced, we all waited in great anticipation to hear the booming of the guns. To our disappointment, the guns were never fired.

In every school there always seemed to be a bully. We must have been lucky at Highland Park, because we had two, Richard and Raymond. The one I had trouble with was Raymond, a surly kid who always wanted to fight. His path home from school was the same as mine and everyday he and his friend would try to goad me into a scrap. For quite a while, I would not be goaded, though there were many inflammatory remarks and even the occasional rock hurled in my direction, until one day when Raymond physically confronted me and started hitting me with the heel of his hand in my chest. Father had always instructed me that it was stupid to fight and to just walk away. But something inside my head snapped after the last poke in the chest. My body was seized with adrenalin and I grabbed him around the head and threw him to the ground. Not letting go, I began to ram Raymond's head into a nearby tree. When I finally let him go, he left, whimpering with his friend. I was not bothered again. This scene was played out graphically in one of my favorite movies, *A Christmas Story*. Coincidentally, the time frame in the movie was in the 1930s, not too long before the foregoing incident took place.

White Center Businesses and Amusements

Walter Coy owned and operated the only theatre in White Center called Coy's Center Theatre. When he first started, he operated out of a storefront space next to Olberg's Drug Store. Later he built a nice theatre on Roxbury St. between 16th and 17th S.W.

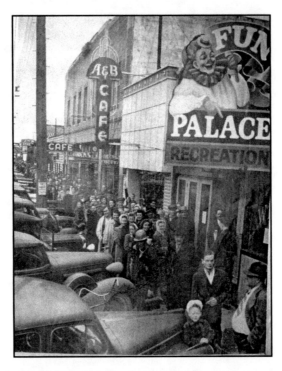

Notes on the back of this picture taken in 1942, on Christmas Day, indicate that the big crowd was waiting to et into Coy's White Center Theater to see Bing Crosby in White Christmas, at that time a big box office draw. It also contains the information that the original White Center Theater was at 9603-16th S.W. and opened on Halloween Day, 1936 (that is, was re-opened, after Coy bought it from George Shrigley.) Many of the same businesses with the same signs are still in their original locations on 16th Avenue. Walter Coy is visible in the doorway under the word Palace.

Coy's White Center Theater in 1947)

Mr. Coy always said his profit margins were better selling popcorn than what he took in through the ticket window. On Saturdays there was a continuing serial that never seemed to end. The hero or heroine was always left in a near-death situation at the end of each episode that prompted one to come the next Saturday to see what happened. Since my friends and I were always short of money, we devised a plan to sneak into the theatre. Located behind the building was an exit near the screen where heavy curtains blocked the light that might come in whenever the door was opened. We would knock on the exit door outside and some kid would sneak over and let us in. Crawling under the seats toward the lobby, we would pop up slowly in some empty seats somewhere in the middle of the theater. This went on for weeks until one day we got caught. We were all hauled up to the lobby, ostensibly to be reprimanded. To our surprise, the big brother of one of our friends was working as the manager. He just talked to us and then let us back into the movie but from then on, we found ways to earn enough money to pay our way.

Oren Artlip had a meat market and grocery store on the N.E. corner of 16th S.W. and 98th Street. He participated in the annual celebrations called White Center Days. Oren would provide a side of beef for roasting over a fire pit, which slowly turned on a spit. Later in the evening it would be carved and served to anyone willing to pay the plate price. With no money in pocket, I was just a drooling bystander.

I attended a small church on Holden Street where Oren taught a Sunday school class. He made us memorize all the books of the Bible and various verses. After I was discharged from the Army in 1951, I enrolled at the University of Washington to study architecture on the GI Bill. I received a stipend of $75 a month for expenses. It was never enough and Oren would let me charge my groceries at his store. At the end of the month when I received my check, I promptly paid him. It was very kind of him to help me through my five years of study in the School of Architecture.

All kinds of events took place during the White Center Days celebration. A boxing ring was set up and participants were encouraged to get into the ring blindfolded, one hand tied behind their back and the other hand was fitted with a 16-ounce boxing glove. It was usually a bunch of younger guys that were coaxed into the ring. When 8 or so volunteers were put together they entered the ring. At the sound of the bell everyone started flailing about trying to knock someone down. Once down, you had to get out of the ring. The last one standing won a monetary prize of around two dollars. One such event I remember well. A kid named Royce Natole was very short and ended up in the ring with some big guys. He was a feisty redhead with a face that was covered with large red freckles. The big guys kept swinging over the top of him. It got down to Royce and one of the big Ridley brothers. Royce couldn't knock the big guy down and Ridley kept flailing the air over his head. He finally took the thumb of his 16-ounce glove and raised his blindfold and then popped Royce with a blow knocking Royce out of the ring.

While Oren's Market was of good size, the surrounding neighborhoods were dotted with Mom and Pop grocery stores. I can think of about eight within a six-block radius of our home. There were no big superstores like we have today so all weekday shopping was done at the store closest to home, which in our case was Martha's Grocery store. Saturdays, however, were reserved for a trip downtown to the Pike Place Market. Years later, the biggest store I'd ever seen was built by Safeway on the corner of 16th and Roxbury. It was the talk of the town for it was the first supermarket with grocery carts and checkout stands and for all of us who only knew the Mom and Pop stores, miles of shelves filled with every food product imaginable. It was new and very special.

There were no television sets or portable phones in those days so we would listen to our favorite radio programs in the evenings. They came one after another over the span of two or three hours—*Terry and the Pirates, Little Orphan Annie, The Shadow, The Green Hornet, Popeye, The Lone Ranger* and many others. It was easy to be so entertained. The wonderful thing about these programs is you had to use your imagination—unlike today where everything is visual. However one program my father wouldn't allow us to listen to was *Gang Busters*. He was opposed to violence of any kind.

At the gas station located just around the corner from our house, a big event to watch was the arrival of the Gilmore gas tanker. The giant truck was highly polished and elaborately decorated with all kinds of banners and flags and pictures of lions. It was like watching the circus roll into town. The driver would employ a great deal of drama as he set out to entertain the crowd of young boys that would gather to watch. He would drag out the hoses and proceed to fill the underground tanks as we kids ran up to touch the truck and marvel at all the colorful banners

The pumps that were used to dispense gas had a glass cylinder with measurements marking the number of gallons set on top of a metal one and gas was pumped by hand up into this glass container so that one could see how much gas he was about to purchase. This had to be done by the mechanic on duty or by one of the ladies working in the grocery store. When the proper measure of fuel appeared, it then flowed by gravity through a hose inserted into your tank or container. The hose formed a loop so when it was put back into the holder, there was always some gas left in the loop of the hose. The pumps were locked up at night, with some gas always left in that loop. This excess fuel caused a near disaster, as I will explain later in my story.

The Salvation Army

One day I walked home alone from the White Center Fieldhouse after a game of basketball. I was heading north on 16th Avenue when I came upon a building with its doors open to the street. As dusk was approaching, the lights inside made it easy to see a variety of power tools arranged throughout the interior. There was a band saw, table saws, planers and other woodworking equipment. I walked up the stairs to get a better look and was peering into the rooms when a friendly face greeted me. I was invited in and asked if I was interested in learning about power tools. The gentleman explained patiently about the various machines. It was the large band saw that got my attention as it allowed one to cut wood into almost any shape desired. I had walked into a Salvation Army program set up to get kids off the street and teach them how to use power tools.

I came back several times to learn about the creative machines and it inspired me to save money so that I could purchase my own tools. I remember my first purchase, a small electric coping saw that worked like a miniature band saw. I bought it from the Ernst Hardware store at the corner of 6th and Pike in downtown Seattle. I still have the little saw and it continues to work just fine. The Salvation Army program was great for helping young boys to think about putting things together with their hands, which in turn it was hoped, would lead to a constructive life.

The Boat

Popular Mechanics was, and still is, a most fascinating periodical for inquisitive minds. At 12 or 13 years of age I was intrigued by the magazine as it was full of inventions, ideas and projects one might build. Thumbing through the pages one day I came across some plans showing how to build an outrigger canoe. It was put together in such a simplistic way that it appeared that anyone could build it. I showed the plans to my friends, Earl and Donny and talked them into building it with me. The only problem was that we had no money to purchase the materials necessary for its construction. We decided to scrounge through the neighborhood to find material. We soon found a house nearby under construction and we devised a plan to make a midnight requisition. At the time, houses were being sheathed with 1x8 shiplap, material which happened to meet our needs exactly. So, late one night we crept onto the construction site and secured enough shiplap to do the job, which amounted to about 4 or 5 pieces 12 feet in length. Donny's dad let us build the boat in his backyard and even set up sawhorses for us. He asked us where we got the lumber and we told him about the good contractor who gave us the lumber because he liked our plan to build a boat. I'm sure Donny's dad took the story with a grain of salt. I think he also believed we would never finish the project, satisfied that it was something constructive and would keep us out of trouble.

We cut the spreaders as shown on the plans and bent the long boards around them where they were brought to points at the bow and stern. The floorboards were cut and nailed perpendicular to the sides. With the outriggers cut and nailed together to the boom, in a couple of weeks it began to look like a boat

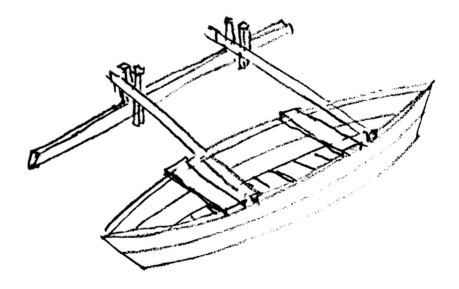

The outrigger canoe

We had no caulking for the seams, which of course would have leaked like a sieve without it. What could be done to resolve this? Someone came up with the idea of using tar. Where to get the tar? Some of the concrete paved streets around our homes had tar poured into the joints. We scoured the neighborhood and found some and began prying the tar out of the cracks in the pavement. It was summer time and the tar was just soft enough to make it relatively easy to pull up. Donny's mother wouldn't let us melt the tar on her kitchen stove, so we built a fire in the backyard and melted the tar in tins. It worked quite well and we poured the hot tar into every seam until the canoe was watertight. It didn't look very good unpainted, however, so Donny's dad gave us the remnants of some old green porch paint which the three of us slopped onto the boat. Finally finished, we stood back to admire our work and all agreed that it looked great. We were ready to christen and launch our handiwork.

Donny's dad refused to put the canoe on the top of his car, a relatively new Buick, and no one had a trailer. We finally talked Earl's dad into putting it on top of his car. The roof was padded with old blankets and with the canoe tied down we headed for Puget Sound. Lincoln Park was close by, where we wouldn't have to carry the canoe very far to reach the water. Sadly, Donny's dad wouldn't let him go with us—he thought it was too dangerous—hence, it was only Earl and I on the maiden voyage. Neither of us could swim so we took an air-filled inner tube as a flotation device in case we capsized. The canoe was put into the water and to everyone's surprise it didn't leak a drop. The outrigger stabilized the craft making it very sturdy in the water. Earl's dad waved us a goodbye and we were off.

There was no plan made for a pickup and neither of us had watches, but we paddled our sleek new canoe out to sea to explore the secrets of Puget Sound. It was a bright, clear summer day and we didn't care if we ever returned. The Fauntleroy ferry terminal was nearby so we paddled our way around the pilings under the dock. The pilings were alive with all kinds of sea life clinging to the surface. Brilliant blue mussel shells in large clusters, thousands of barnacles and further down we could see giant purple and orange colored starfish with their arms wrapped tightly to the encrusted supports. We tried to pry them off with our paddles but couldn't quite reach them. There were all kinds of fish swimming amongst the pilings and we were upset that we didn't bring a fishing line. We paddled for several hours until the sun began to go down when we decided to head for shore. We pulled the boat up on a stretch of sandy beach in front of a private home. I went to the door and asked the lady if it would be all right to leave our canoe on her beach and that we would be back next weekend to pick it up. She said that would be fine, but that we should be sure to tie it up well. We followed her advice and proceeded to walk home.

The next weekend we were excited about going to sea again and Earl's dad drove us to the park. We ran down to the beach to load up our gear but the canoe was nowhere in sight. After searching for a while we found a part of the green bow protruding from the sand. The boat was completely buried among the rocks and sand as, evidently, some large waves swamped it and the action of the water proceeded to destroy our beautifully built project. Dejected, we said goodbye to it and went home, thus ending our first adventure with the sea.

Swamps

Before developers started building houses to meet the demands of migrants arriving to work in the war industries (shipyards, aircraft building, etc.), there were great swamps everywhere around White Center. Eventually, development filled them in but surface drainage continued to collect in every swale and depression. There was a swamp in the woods next door to our house and over the hill to the east were several swamps and there were two great swamps next to our Highland Park Grade School.

To a young boy, a swamp is about the greatest place in the world to explore. It is a marvel of microscopic life from pollywogs to frogs. Like Columbus setting sail into the unknown, one could tie some logs together, make a raft and set off to explore. The green gooey masses of algae were pulled back to see what lay below. Frogs were caught and brought home for further examination. You could get a plasma-like mass of frog eggs and watch them hatch into pollywogs or you could catch a jar full of pollywogs and watch them grow. The joy of a having a swamp nearby, however, was a constant worry to our parents as they were sure we would fall in and drown. We did fall in on many occasions and would come home soaking wet with green slime hanging from our pants and over our shoes. Whenever we went out to play we would be told, "Stay out of the swamps!"

One day, coming home slimy and wet, I stole into the basement, took off all my clothes and hung them to dry above the metal smoke stack that led from the wood burning furnace. The furnace was not fired up so I thought it was safe to leave them hang there and after a few days I forgot about them. The weather turned colder and in the dark my Dad, unaware that my clothes were hanging close to the smoke stack, fired up the furnace. I was off playing away from the house and heard the roar of sirens and fire engines. I thought, "Oh boy—a fire!" and I ran to follow the sound of the engines.

I was shocked to see them all standing in front of our house. The clothing hanging over the furnace pipe had ignited and started to burn the floor joists. My bother called the fire department, but my Dad had already rushed into the basement with a bucket of water to quickly douse the flames before the fire department arrived. I was instructed to never hang clothing near those pipes again, and… to stay out of the swamps!

The swamp next to the grade school was an ongoing project for our science class. We gathered frog eggs along with buckets of swamp water and put them in a large container in the classroom. Each day we made our observations of the progress and soon had frogs that we released back into the swamp. We were fortunate to have access to this living laboratory as all kinds of lessons were learned there.

Recently, I read an article about swamps and wetlands that described them as "the kidneys of the land." Swamps take in all sorts of harmful pollutants and chemicals and break them down to be assimilated by other living organisms. All the swamps mentioned above are gone now—filled in with housing developments built over them. I don't think anyone at the time realized what they were doing. These swamps were such an important part of the local ecosystem.

In White Center, Mr. Neupert was the owner of Neupert's Market located on the corner of Roxbury and Delridge Way. He had one glass eye and looking up at him could be a very uncomfortable experience. I would focus on his glass eye, which at times rotated slightly and would appear to be staring off in a sideways direction while his good eye was looking right at me. My own eyes began to cross, trying to maintain eye contact with him would make me dizzy. Mr. Neupert was a big, burly man and though he appeared intimidating, he was very gentle of heart. He was also our Scoutmaster, as he loved working with kids.

After the WWII started it was impossible to find any decent candy, especially chocolate bars. As a grocery store owner, Mr. Neupert always had a case of Hershey bars. On our scout outings, he would organize contests and the winners always got a chocolate bar. Being a confirmed chocoholic, I won my fair share by competing furiously in those contests.

Mr. Neupert loved to tell stories and was very good at it. In the evenings around the campfire, he and his wandering eye would start spinning tales. The stories would have us hypnotized and at their climax, completely terrified. One of his favorites was *The Man With The Golden Arm*. Some details escape me now, but it had to do with a man coming back from the dead looking for his lost arm. Mr. Neupert would bob and weave amongst us while telling the story and then suddenly he would spin and bellow "Gotcha!" as we sat on pins and needles. It is a wonder any of us slept after such a story night.

Snowy Winters

During the 1930s and into the 1940s Seattle had snow every winter. Not always at Christmas but through the winter months there was usually plenty of the white stuff. The hills around our home provided great opportunities for sledding, but most of our parents could not afford to buy sleds. Ingenuity prevailed and sleds were made of two boards that were crudely fashioned into the runners. With our father's help we were able to make nice, rounded tips on the runners, then added a piece of plywood across the top to hold the runners together. The sled worked, but the bottom edge of the runners could not provide the frictionless ride of a steel runner, hence they were not as fast as the store-bought kind.

Over the hill from us was the location of a huge dump. All the refuse collected in the city of Seattle was brought to this site, between 1st Avenue South and Kenyon streets. Here the marshlands formed by the wanderings of the Duwamish River were being filled with the city's garbage. The material that could be burned was set afire creating huge billows of smoke until, at times, it resembled a burning oil field. Smoke covered the area known as South Park. The fires burned day and night all year long. Sometimes paint and oil and rubber tires were thrown into the inferno causing the smoke to become black and acrid. The people of the South Park area complained to the city fathers to no avail and in those days I'm sure that the paints used were all lead-based. What a task the EPA would have had if it had existed then!

For kids however, the dump was a fascinating place to explore. We could shoot rats with BB guns and collect all kinds of discarded, but still useful items. Among these were the steel bandings that were used to hold wooden crates together. This banding was the perfect material for the aforementioned runners on our wooden sleds. It was about half an inch in width and could be easily nailed to the runners. While our homemade sleds could not possibly compete with the racy, store-bought models, we never stopped trying.

A block away from our home was the 11th Avenue hill known to all sledders as the best place to race. There was one year that I managed to beat the other kids. In my scavenging I had located some thin steel rods that were about a quarter inch in diameter and with a neighbor's help they were bent and fastened around the wooden runner bottoms with counter-sunk screws. The sled had a low profile and looked very sleek. We even cut some slots through tops of the runners to create grips so we could get a better hold and hence a better running start. The only way to steer the sled, however, was to drag your left or right foot depending on which direction you wanted to go. It was a beautiful racing machine and all my friends wanted to ride it. I was even able to trade rides with some of the kids who owned store-bought sleds. Their sleds had the advantage of steering handles, but mine was very fast in a straight line.

One day someone brought a toboggan to the hill. The one bad thing about this hill was that there were always a number of stalled cars that we had to dodge around on the way down. Toboggans can hold several kids at a time, but are difficult to steer, especially for amateurs. No matter, a group of us jumped on and away we went, trying frantically to stay in the center of the road, only to lose control and crash into a parked car. There were some cracked heads and a broken arm. The "great toboggan crash" was talked about for many days. The terrible toboggan was finally banned from the hill and the incident brought about parent-supervised sledding, which every kid knows is no fun at all. Though we hoped and prayed that the snow would last for weeks, in a few days it always disappeared.

The Bus Shack

Martha's Corner Grocery Store at 9th and Kenyon was also a gas station, a precursor of the many handy-marts of today. I was delivering the morning paper, the Seattle Post-Intelligencer, and in the winter the weather would chill me to bone while I folded the papers into a roll that could be thrown from the street onto a porch without unraveling. The papers were delivered to a bus shelter across the street from the store. Unpacking our bundles of papers always generated a great deal of waste paper and we would burn the scrap along with bits of wood in a 50-gallon barrel steel drum.

On one exceptionally cold, snowy morning we decided that we needed a bigger fire. The extra sticks we threw into the drum were too damp and the fire only sputtered and died. Across the street at the gas station, we had discovered that the gas pump hoses retained some gas after each use. We found some tin cans and filled them up, dumped them into barrel and tossed in a match. The ensuing explosion shot a flame fifty feet into the air. We weren't hurt, but we stood paralyzed with fear for we had parted the power lines above. That was the last time we tried that stunt.

Some time later we moved our paper folding and fire drum into a bus stop shelter that was constructed by neighborhood volunteers. The early morning bus riders enjoyed the warmth of our fire as they waited for the bus and every morning when we finished folding papers, we would douse the fire, muscle the smoking drum out of the shelter and leave to make our deliveries. Unfortunately some undetected embers fell into the cracks between the wooden floor planks of the shelter which set the bus stop on fire. An alert neighbor called the fire department and the shelter was saved, but that was the end of our hand-warming fires.

My Friend Bill, aka Robert

At various times I had delivered the Seattle Star, the Seattle Times and the P.I. The Star was my favorite because it had the best comic strips. The one I liked the most was *Alley Oop*, who was a cave man with a pet dinosaur named Dinny. In the strip, he also had a scientist friend named Doc who invented a time machine for time travel into the past. Alley Oop was brought into present day life with the time machine. Alley Oop's legs became larger as they progressed downward from his knees so that his ankles appeared to be larger than his thighs—a good solid base. My pal, Bill Clarke, had legs similar to Alley Oops, but not quite as thick as the comic character's. For years we played basketball, football, baseball and tennis at the White Center Fieldhouse and Highland Park Playfield, so Bill's legs were well developed. My mother, who was a wonderful cook, made a meat-filled bun called a *pirozhok*. This is a delightful, traditional Russian dish and all of the kids in the neighborhood loved them. They would stand in line at the back porch awaiting a handout Saturday evenings when my mother prepared them. Mother liked Bill Clarke and because he was so skinny (save for his legs), she saw to it that he was well fed.

Several years later, while serving in the Army during the Korean War, I was in transit to the Far East. Two weeks after the start of the war, I landed at Fairfield Susin Air Force Base in California. Here soldiers would board four-engine, propeller driven, civilian planes chartered from Northwest Airlines by the military to be flown to Japan. The day before we arrived at the base, General Travis was killed in an airplane crash on the field. Later, the base was renamed Travis Air Force Base, but immediately following the crash, the field was covered with debris and the ongoing investigation delayed the movement of troops. The place was in turmoil with planes backed up and thousands of troops milling around in the lobby waiting to be sent overseas. Military personnel were sleeping and sitting on the floor as all available chairs and sofas were occupied.

I made a trip to the base bathroom filled with enlisted men and so I had to wait in line for a stall while guys were shaving and cleaning up. I observed a person who was in a stall changing his trousers and I could see his bare legs from under the stall wall. I had to look twice and I said to myself, there could only be one guy in the world with legs like that. I said, "Bill, is that you?" It turned out it was, and though he didn't have much time to talk then, he told me that he had joined the Navy and was to be shipped out to the Far East for carrier duty. Recently we got together and relived a lot of old stories, including the Alley Oop legs. Bill pulled his pant leg up and said, "See, they don't look so bad." I think the "muscle" in his legs had moved to other parts of his body, notably his midsection.

The kids from White Center were generally known as a tough bunch. Bill dropped out of West Seattle High and after getting himself into some kind of trouble his dad gave him two choices—join the Navy or go to reform school. Bill signed with the Navy and served four years. After discharge, he took advantage of the GI Bill and went back to school to get his high school diploma and continued on to college where he received bachelor and master's degrees and finally a doctorate in English Literature. He is now a retired professor from the University of West Virginia and living in Buckhannon, West Virginia where he writes a gad fly column for the local newspaper. His column is titled *BOB CLARKE Curmudgeon's Corner.*

Bill told me about one of his experiences on the carrier during the Korean War. As a deck hand, he worked on the flight deck assisting takeoffs and landings. One day an officer thought Bill should work below decks in the area that controlled the flow of fuel from the storage tanks to the flight deck. Though as Bill puts it, "I am not necessarily mechanically inclined," they put him in a room filled with valves, meters, pumps and gauges. With these items adorning all of the wall space, the seaman in charge told Bill he was going on deck to have a smoke. Just as soon as the seaman had left, an order came down to send fuel up to the flight deck. In a panic, Bill looked around the room for the right valves, levers or buttons to activate the flow and took a wild guess. Six jets were fueled with seawater before someone realized what was happening. The following day Bill was back on the flight deck and the seaman in charge was severely reprimanded for leaving a novice in charge of the fuel room. Today bill goes by his real first name, Robert.

The Holidays

The Easter celebration for the Russian Orthodox faith is more important than the Christmas holiday. Mom would start preparing various dishes more than a week in advance. This usually involved a special trip to the Pike Place Market. Either my brother or I would help mom on this shopping expedition. The market in the 1930s and 40s was primarily selling food products. There were various vendors that were my mom's favorite. At the meat market mom bought pig's knuckles and veal for making *holadetz,* a jellied veal dish served on Easter with horseradish. The horseradish we grew in the backyard and I would help my dad run it through a grater. This caused tears to run down our faces. I soon learned that fresh horseradish is more potent than slicing onions.

In the market after the meat was purchased we wound our way down the stairs to the spice shop. I loved it there because the aroma of the spices reminded me of the seafaring tales that I had been reading about.

The spice shop was dimly lit and the wooden floor squeaked as we walked across the boards giving the feeling of being on a ship. Mom purchased saffron here to mix with the dough that was to make the *kulichi,* Russian Easter cakes. One cake would be selected to be blessed by the priest at the Russian Orthodox Church to be served at the Easter feast. The top of the *kulichi* was frosted and decorated with spreckles and candies. The cakes were baked in the oven in tubular tins that varied in diameter and height. It was disappointing to see the cakes laid sideways when cut because we looked forward to getting some of the frosting. Pieces were cut below the frosting cap and served to each guest. The cake was stood back upright and the frosted cap reset on top of the remaining portion. The frosted top was the last to be eaten. Mom would then cut it up and divide it into portions for each of the siblings.

We did not have a mechanical dough mixer. The mixing for the cake dough had to be done by hand. I volunteered to help and soon realized what a difficult job it was. Mom had done this year after year—always by hand. The dough had to be brought to a certain texture and consistency. Mom kept checking on my mixing and it seemed like an hour before she said *horosho,* good in Russian.

The next stop at the market was at the fishmonger's. In front of his fish case there was a large wooden barrel filled with salted herring. Mom would peer in and make her selection. At home the salted herring would be placed in a pan of water to leach out the excess salt. This was an overnight process. The herring would be cut into small bits and served with slices of hard-boiled egg garnished with parsley—a colorful dish. These hors d'oeuvres were usually served with ice-cold vodka.

Mom had two favorite butchers, one was near the Pike Street entrance and the other was at the opposite end on the Desimone Bridge. This was the near last stop of our shopping so the heavy items were purchased here—a ham with the bone in and a roast or a turkey. The butcher would always throw in some soup bones for free.

At home the ham was highly decorated with cloves, brown sugar and pineapples. The pig feet, veal and vegetables were boiled with spices. Mom would let me separate the meat from the bone of the pig knuckles. I loved this job because when I finished I had a pile of bones that I savored—sucking out the marrow and chewing the softened cartilage. Helping Mom in the kitchen was always enjoyable for me.

The very last stop at the market was the Fairmont Dairy. Here mom purchased items for making *paska*, a very rich dessert made with eggs, butter, sugar, cheese, almonds and fresh vanilla that was also purchased at the spice shop. The mixture was placed into cheesecloth then pressed into a wooden mold that was shaped like a pyramid. My dad had made this mold. On top there was a wood block that fit into the base of the pyramid. The pyramid which had a flat top was turned upside-down, placed into a sink and a stone weight was placed on the wood block. This insured that all the excess moisture would drain out.

The Fairmont Dairy churned their own butter and made their own ice cream. The shopping trip always ended with a freshly made dish of ice cream. My favorite was a vanilla strawberry made with fresh strawberries.

The Easter table was a sight to behold with all of the week's preparations in a colorful display. As guests came in, they oohed and aahed at my mother's beautiful table. Prayers were said and toasts were made and everyone sat down to a sumptuous Easter feast.

My father who had been in the czar's military taught my brother and me how to excuse ourselves from the table if we wanted to make an exit. We would get up from the table, go to each guest, bow and with a click of the heels, ask to be excused. My sisters followed the same procedure but curtsied in place of bowing.

At Christmastime a tree was put up and decorated. A great deal of lead foil tinsel was used along with ornaments of all shapes and sizes, garlands and strings of lights. My mother took a great deal of time to tie loops around candy-coated animal crackers and hang them on the tree. These were not to be touched until Christmas Day. Stockings were hung above the fireplace with great anticipation of St. Nick's arrival. There was always a star at the top of the tree with a red light. The tree was also festooned with real wax candles that were seated in a metal disk with a clamp that one could attach to a branch. As I recall, the candles were never lit.

In the living room near the tree was an old-fashioned rocking chair that my dad had reupholstered with a red velvety material. My brother and I loved to rock each other in this chair. Once, when it was my turn, my brother started gently rocking me. I said, "Rock harder!" and he did. In fact, he rocked me so hard that the chair went over backwards and as I flew out of it my airborne feet hooked garlands in the tree and everything came down with a violent crash. My mother rushed in and was horrified to see me under the tree decorated with garlands and icicles. As I recall she did not yell at us but quickly set about resetting the tree and decorations before my dad got home. My brother and I quietly helped mom restore the tree to its original glory. Not a word was mentioned to my dad so we did not get punished for our exuberant behavior.

Sex Education

Sex education at home and at school was absolutely nil. Everything you

41

learned about girls came in the form of stories told and retold, which at each telling became exaggerated. At the start of the war, many families from Montana and the Dakotas moved west to work at Boeing or in the shipyards. There were a lot of strange kids living in the area and some lived on small farms. Bestiality was something I never understood or, really, ever will. This story was told to me by one of the participants and I will call him Dale for the purposes of anonymity. Dale told me how after milking his cow he would stand on his milking stool and have intercourse with "Bessie." One evening a bunch of us guys got together and were retelling this story. Geno, who was hard of hearing, blurted out that "It wouldn't be so bad as long as the cow didn't roll over on you." Geno only heard the part about the intercourse with the cow and not the part about standing on the stool. The vision of someone rolling in the hay with a cow was just too much and we couldn't stop laughing. We reminded Geno of his for years to come.

One of my friends, Danny, used to work for Mr. Neupert as a stock boy. The war years took most of the young men into various branches of the military, leaving mostly young boys and old men. A young lady, working at the store always tried to get Danny into a situation where she could put the make on him. There was only one bathroom on the premises and this young lady would leave the door unlocked whenever she used it. One day, Danny had to go to the restroom and walked in to find her waiting. She invited him in and told him to lock the door. He was so startled by this very forward confrontation that he stammered apologies and left, flushed with embarrassment. Later a similar incident happened to me while working at the New Washington Hotel dining room. As teenagers, we were just a naive bunch of kids who fell into situations with lonely women. We were taught nothing about the opposite sex at home or at school.

To satisfy the libido that dominated our teen years, Herby and some of his friends organized a club they called The Jack-Off Club. They would secret themselves off in nearby the woods for the purpose of masturbating. The one who ejaculated the furthest was crowned the winner. To this day I do not know who was the winner as I was not a member of this erectile organization. However, a very unfortunate thing happened to Herby in the course of this activity. I am not a medical expert, but as Herby explained it, while he was masturbating once too often on the downward stroke, he tore the ligaments or chords that left his penis looking like a broken banana. This was very serious since every time he had an erection, he had what looked like a curled cucumber. Later, when Herby got married, he related the great difficulty he encountered while trying to have sex with his wife. He attempted every position imaginable, known to man, to fulfill his conjugal obligations and I must confess, some of his positions sounded exciting. It was decided that he should see a doctor. An operation was performed and his life was literally straightened out. All is well that ends well!

Daisy

There was a very sexually active girl living two doors to the south of our house. I will call her Daisy. She was friendly and she lived with her Grandmother who never seemed to be at home. There were boys coming and going to visit Daisy at all hours. One day, Daisy asked me to take pictures of her and a girlfriend. She produced a camera and after a few snapshots, she asked me for one of the two of us together. Her friend took the camera and Daisy snuggled up against my body to make sure I was aware of all her charms. Instantly aroused, I had to put my hand in my pocket to conceal my budding manhood. The camera ran out of film and we all went into the house for more film. The film, for some reason, was in the bedroom and we were all sitting on the bed reloading the camera. Daisy's girlfriend reached into her blouse and undid her bra. It was at that moment that I heard my mother calling me to dinner. I excused myself and, keeping my hand in my pocket, hobbled home. Mother saved my virginity. Thanks Mom, but there's more to Daisy.

We always played football on a vacant lot below our property. We would keep playing even into darkness. One evening, Daisy came over and wanted to join in. We explained the game of tackle football and she was eager to play. Everyone agreed that Daisy should carry the ball. Daisy was tackled on each carry by everyone. After we'd finished playing one of the guys asked me, "Did you cop a feel?" I didn't know what he was talking about but learned later that she thoroughly enjoyed being groped each time she carried the ball. Daisy asked all of us to stop by her place the next evening. On my way home I was passing her house and she was on the porch. She asked me where everyone was and she invited me in for a soda pop. She was telling me what a rough game football is and how she was covered with black and blue marks and would I like to see them? I declined, finished my soda and went home.

The War Starts

I was eleven years old when United States became involved in World War II. December 7, 1941 was a beautiful morning and I was playing in the yard. My parents were in the house entertaining a German friend, Mr. Eckhard, whom they had known for many years. Mr. Eckhard liked his cigars and as I remember, always had one in his mouth, lit or unlit. He was a stout man with a round, balding head and he wore thick glasses. He spoke with a very thick accent and if you were near him, all you could smell was stale cigar smoke.

My parents and Mr. Eckhard were discussing the war in Europe when suddenly, Jackie Moore, a neighbor came running across a vacant field where we played ball shouting, "The Japs have bombed Pearl Harbor! We're at war!" I didn't know what or where Pearl Harbor was, but I ran into the house to relay the news. Upon hearing this, my parents and Mr. Eckhard all hugged each other and began to cry. The radio was quickly turned on and sure enough, every station was filled with news and reassurances from President Franklin Roosevelt that we would prevail.

The war was already well under way in Europe and my parents had relatives living in Latvia. My dad's brother and his family and a sister on my mother's side, along with some cousins, as well as some relatives in China who were preparing to leave for Australia, were all trapped by Hitler's and Hirohito's advancing armies. The news hit home and hit hard. But to a young mind, the war was a million miles away. While we went on playing our kid games, the sense of alarm in the adults around us let us know that this was something very big. My parents knew about the trauma of war first hand. They had left Russia just as the Revolution got under way in 1917 and fled to China ahead of the advancing Red Army. From China they were able to immigrate to the United States. With most of our relatives still in Latvia and other parts of Europe, the daily news of Hitler's movements weighed on us heavily.

After the war was over, we learned that my Dad's brother Kolya was killed by Russian bombs in a rail yard where he worked. He was trying to avoid being hit and dove under a boxcar, which was then struck directly by a bomb. We got the news from his son, Lev, who was an engineer and was forced to work for the Germans. He ended up in a British displaced persons camp in a zone occupied by the British. When the war ended there was a great deal of letter writing and my parents were able to get Lev and his mother to the U.S. Another brother of my father was living in London and survived the severe bombing of that city.

During the war years, I continued delivering newspapers. The first months of the war produced reams of terribly depressing news. With Germans advancing all over Europe, Africa and Russia, the Japanese advancing throughout the Pacific and invading the Philippines, the depressing news seemed like it would never end. Bataan and Corrigedor fell and horrible things were happening to allied prisoners there. Singapore fell on February 15, 1942 with the capture of 130,000 Allied troops. Our ships were being sunk in various sea battles throughout the South Pacific and the British battleships *Repulse* and *Prince of Wales* were sunk by Japanese aircraft on December 10th of that year. There was bad news about the Battle of the Java Sea and Darwin, a northern Australian port, was attacked.

As time passed, things slowly began to turn for the Allies. There was the April 18th surprise raid on Tokyo by the Doolittle Raiders from the carrier the *USS Hornet*. The Battle of The Coral Sea was a standoff, but it stopped the Japanese from invading Port Moresby, Australia in that same month. Then came the Battle of Midway on June 3, 1942 that turned out to be the turning point of the war.

I remember delivering a newspaper with large black letters on the front page. The date was June 4, 1942 and the headline read JAPS BOMB DUTCH HARBOR. Having never heard of Dutch Harbor, I soon learned that it was in Alaska and a palpable fear gripped the Northwest.

Would Seattle be next?

Severe black outs were ordered. The streetlight bulbs were all painted black except for a slit at the underside where the lights could continue to illuminate at a fraction of their original capacity. The same was done on the headlights of all cars and trucks in the area, so at night time the lamps shone eerily through narrow slots. Air raid wardens patrolled the neighborhoods to make sure that not even a trickle of light was leaking out from behind the blackout shades in each home. Seattle slipped into darkness.

My father volunteered to be an air raid warden for our block and was issued a helmet, a gas mask and a portable fire extinguisher for putting out incendiary bombs that might be dropped. The Japanese tried this tactic by attaching bombs to gas-filled balloons that were set adrift from the Japanese mainland to catch the jet stream across the Pacific Ocean. To my knowledge little or no damage ever occurred from these devices.

While our parents fretted about the war, life for us kids continued with the usual ball games. Returning from an evening of basketball at the White Center Fieldhouse, during an exceptionally foggy night, with the blackout still in effect the whole area was pitch dark and spooky. I decided to play a trick on the three friends I was with. I made an excuse that I had to be home early and then ran on ahead into the darkness. I climbed into a tree where I knew my friends would soon be passing under. In the murkiness, three figures soon came into view. As they strolled beneath me, I grabbed a limb and with a Tarzan-like scream, I came flying out of the dark and landed on the ground in front of them. Looking back now, I don't know who was more terrified—me or the three black kids I had dropped on top of. The boys, who were bigger than me, shouted and one yelled, "Jesus Christ man!" and all took off running into the fog. Moments later my friends showed up and when I told them what had happened we all laughed. I felt lucky to be alive.

From the White Center Fieldhouse there were two ways to get home. One was by following the roads and the second was a shortcut over a large swampy area that extended north from the Fieldhouse and on past Roxbury Street. There was a large pipe about 18 inches in diameter that carried water to the Highland Park Reservoir across the swamp. The pipe rested on large concrete blocks about three feet above the water line. It was a challenge to walk this pipe during the day, but it shortened the walk home by several blocks. On one misty night we decided to walk the pipe home. A sign saying "Slippery When Wet" would have been helpful, because I ended up with the distinction of being the only one to fall off into the swamp.

Going to High School

To get to West Seattle High School we caught a bus at the crest of Highland Park Way (called Boeing Hill). Bus fare was two tokens for a nickel—one for the ride to school and one for the ride home. The bus wound it's way south to White Center, turned west on Roxbury and then north on 35th S.W. to Alaska, to California Avenue and then to the school. By the time we made all the stops and arrived at school, the bus was packed and there was standing room only. The ride was nearly an hour and a half long. You can't pack that many teenagers into the confines of a bus and expect them to sit quietly the entire time, so over the months and years, various mischievous deeds were concocted to break the boredom of the ride.

There was the squirt gun phase where more water was flying around in the bus than in rainstorms outside. Not to be outdone by mere dime-store squirt guns, I took a bicycle pump and filled it with about a half quart of water. It worked perfectly. My mistake was in underestimating the distance capabilities of the makeshift water cannon. Sitting about two thirds back from the front of the bus, I let a discharge of H^2O fly towards the passengers in the front and ended up hitting the driver in the back of the head. The bus slammed to a halt so fast that all the people standing were squeezed into the front of the vehicle. The soaked driver jumped from his seat and with the demeanor of a raging bull worked his way toward the back looking for the culprit who plastered him. The only thing that saved me was the fact that I was so far back, he assumed that since the shot came from directly behind him, it had to have been done by someone sitting nearby—the cheap, plastic squirt guns didn't have the range that my cannon did. His failed search was my good fortune .

Another adventure was the "dismantling" of the bus. I can honestly say that I did not participate in this activity, but someone discovered that a dime would fit perfectly into the slots of the screws that held the windows. With the screws removed, the windows were taken out and tossed out onto the streets as the bus rumbled on. There were so many kids along this route that it required three buses to get us all to school. I always caught the first bus and it was advantageous to be at the first pick up point because a seat was always available. Though we lived at the edge of Rat City, the young people from White Center proper were really a rowdy bunch. I heard of many wild episodes that occurred on the second and third buses such as—"Did you hear what happened on the second bus? They took a girl's clothes off!" or "They built a fire in the back of the third bus today!"

Of course, all of this was reported to the principal and letters would be sent out to all the parents. In most cases we knew who were the perpetrators, but no one dared to rat on them out for fear of reprisal. Our parents admonished us, but we just denied everything saying, "It was those bad kids from White Center that caused all the trouble!"

In 1946, a friend of mine, Gene Mankinen, invited me to go with him to Boeing Field. The war had just ended and his father was the founder of the Puget Sound Flying Service. At 16 years, visiting the airfield was a big deal. The Puget Sound Flying Service was a school that taught flying. With many servicemen coming home with the GI Bill providing education, a lot of them signed up to learn how to fly. Gene and I wandered among the planes all standing in rows. Gene picked one out and said, "You wanna get in?" With my fascination for all aircraft, I said, "SURE!" Sitting in the plane just chatting, Gene monkeyed with the knobs and suddenly reached over and started the engine. He feigned a look of surprise as he taxied the plane out and taxied to the edge of the runway. He radioed the control tower and before I could mutter a protest, we were taking off.

Up we went over Lake Washington. Gene proceeded to terrorize me with barrel rolls and loop-de-loops and other maneuvers. It took a while to relax and for me to realize that Gene really did know how to fly. It turned out that he had just received his pilot's license and that his dad had been teaching him for quite some time before he became eligible for that license. It was a beautiful day and we cruised around and about the city and landed at an airfield that was located in what is now part of Bellevue just off I-90. The field no longer exists and the strip is now covered with buildings. We stepped out of the plane and went into an office, had a coke. It was then when he came clean about the surprise he'd pulled on me. We drank our cokes and hopped back into the plane and after some more acrobatics over Lake Washington, we returned to Boeing Field. When my parents asked me where I had been all day, I told them, "Flying." To my disappointment, no one believed me and admonished me for making up stories.

My father did not drive a car. We had a car that he tried to drive, but for some reason he had great deal of trouble with the stick shift. He had purchased it from a Russian friend who owned Washington Auto Wrecking and it was in perfect condition. A 1932 Chrysler four-door sedan, royal blue with large, nickel chrome headlamps mounted on the front fenders, the auto had been kept in storage. Dad purchased the car for $25 at the beginning of the war. When gas rationing began, he was given an A-card, which was the lowest on the priority list. Dad carpooled to his job at Boeing with a neighbor and gave his ration coupon to him to insure that they had enough gas to get to work. So the car sat in the garage for the entire war, but we would turn the engine over occasionally to make sure it still ran. When my brother Leon learned to drive during his senior year of high school, he and I got to use the car to go to school. It was a classic and it stood out among the other cars.

We played a lot of tennis on a court at Highland Park Playfield. The games went until dark or until we just couldn't see anymore. At Highland Park Grade School there was a gymnasium and we always wished we could get in to play basketball after darkness curtailed our tennis. I don't remember who thought of it, but we decided to try to break into the gym one evening.

The doors were locked and the windows were covered with heavy wire screens. Bill Campbell, who was part Indian, had a remarkable ability to climb nearly anything. Particularly brick buildings, he somehow gripped the mortar joints and quickly scaled up to the wire-screened window. We discovered that the screen could be pulled away from the window, which had friction-style swivel latches. With two of us holding the screen back, Billy wiggled the window up and down until the latch rotated open.

Billy wiggled the window.

He then jumped in and ran to the door and let us all in. We found the basketballs in the office and played to our hearts content until Lyle, the custodian, caught us. Lyle wanted to know how we got in and we told him the door was open and we'd just walked in. He was not much older than us and didn't really care that we were there, just concerned about his freshly swept gym floor. We told him we would sweep up after ourselves and he left us a 3-foot sweeper and each night before we left we would sweep the floor clean. In order to get back in easily, we left the latch undone in the window and no one was ever the wiser.

Eventually the school administration found out about our nighttime activity and we were interrogated as to how we got in. All of us just said the door was open. They insisted that one of us had a key, which we all denied. From that point on, the strangest array of locks began to appear on the door. We kept returning night after night. The interrogations continued, each of us repeating the same story, the door was unlocked. Because the door was a required exit from the gym, it was unlocked from the inside. The administrators finally gave up and said we could use the gym albeit with adult supervision. With a grumpy adult watching us, it was no longer fun and we gave up going to play basketball there. No one ever discovered how we got in. The old brick building is no more and we still revel in the memory of outwitting the powers that be.

Before the old school was replaced, I had the opportunity to re-visit the old stomping grounds as an adult. Newspapers reported that the wife of the Russian president, Boris Yeltsin was going to visit the school, as it was the only school in the region that was teaching the Russian language at the grade school level. I brought my camera and upon my arrival, I was confronted by all sorts of security people who were not going to let me in. I told them that I had attended the school and that my parents were Russian and that I had a right to be there. They relented, checked my I.D. and gave me a name card. Mrs. Yeltsin arrived in a limousine along with a cavalcade of other cars and motorcycle policemen. I had never seen so many people gathered around that school. Mrs. Yeltsin was wearing a bright blue dress and was very gracious. She greeted the children and watched a play. She was given a gift from the school and then was whisked away by her entourage. I did get some pictures and tried to get close enough to speak with her, but was only able to offer a salutation as she left saying, *"Shaslevee Pootee!"* which means "Happy Roads!" She turned and waved and was gone.

At 14 or 15 years of age, I was able to land a job bussing dishes at The New Washington Hotel dining room and coffee shop. The hotel was located on the corner of 2nd and Stewart. It wasn't hard to get work because most adult men were in the military or working in war factories. I told my employer I was 16, but all he was interested in was if I could lift a metal tray filled with dirty dishes. I was skinny and weighed maybe 130 pounds, but I showed them I could do it by carrying a big tray full of dishes to the dumbwaiter with no trouble. The main kitchen and all the dishwashing facilities were in the basement.

The great part of this job was that I could eat all I wanted. To a teenager in the war years, this was a real treat. Also, there was an attractive waitress that took a liking to me and when I helped her clean tables, she shared her tips with me. She was always telling me that, "I bet you would wiggle nice." I was too naïve then to figure out what she was talking about. It was years later that I understood—too late.

I worked the dinner shift and it was a long bus ride from West Seattle to the hotel and a long bus ride back home. The war was dragging on and blackouts were still in effect. Coming home one particularly foggy night, the bus driver was having difficulty negotiating his way to White Center. The First Avenue South Bridge was a rickety two-lane affair over the Duwamish River. It rested on a turntable structure that was in the middle of the river. When opened for water traffic, the bridge pivoted on the turntable until it was parallel with the river. To get onto the ramp leading to the bridge there was a sharp left turn and then at the top there was a sharp right turn onto the bridge. Arriving at the bridge, the fog was even thicker and with the painted headlights and dimmed streetlights, we couldn't even see a yard in front of the bus. The driver asked one of the passengers to get out of the bus and guide him across the bridge with a flashlight. Everyone breathed a sigh of relief when we made it to the other side.

Boeing Before the War

Before the war started the Boeing Company was building the China Clipper ships at their Plant No. 1 at the foot of Boeing hill (Highland Park Way). The China Clipper ships were amphibian aircraft, many flown by Pan American Airways throughout the Pacific. The Duwamish waterway has changed dramatically over the years, but where the Clipper ships were assembled there were tidal flats on three sides of the hangar. North of the hangar doors was a ramp that sloped gently to the water. The airplanes would be taken down the ramp into the Duwamish River where they were floated to Elliott Bay for testing. Across the hangar to the west were a number of houseboats. This was one of our favorite places to play and watch the work progress on the airplanes. When there was a minus tide we could walk across the flats to the hangar. We did this to pick up shiny little scraps of aluminum scattered about in the muck. The red brick buildings of a once very active area are still there, standing in ghostly silence. The Red Barn was relocated to be part of the new Flight Museum located on East Marginal Way.

The Duwamish River delta was very much affected by tides in Puget

Sound. There were marshes with cattails that extended far to the south. People lived in houseboats located on the various fingers of water that extended from the main body of the river. Some were abandoned and we would play in them. When the tide was out the houseboats tilted at very precarious angles. I often wondered how people lived in them with the daily tide changes. Today most of the marshlands are gone along with countless ducks and other wild fowl that used to land there on their way south. One can still see some remaining marshes where Highway 509 meets the 1st Avenue Bridge.

The Boeing 314 Flying Boat weighed 40 tons and cost $550,000. Pan Am had ordered six of the newer 314A models. With WWII starting, only three 314As went to Pan Am. The rest went to the British government. A flight from Washington, D.C. to Marseilles, via the Azores and Lisbon took 29 hours. The 314 carried Winston Churchill on various intercontinental journeys. The area where the plant once stood has completely changed. A recent visit revealed the only remaining aforementioned brick buildings.

Martha's Corner Grocery

At the grocery store near our house, Martha always greeted me in a loud, but friendly voice. She had a harelip and her voice had a nasal twang. She sounded as if she were talking through a pipe. "Hellllthooooo Thathy!" ("Sassy" from Sasonoff) she would shout, but she had a habit of stretching it out over five or ten seconds. She never addressed me by my first name, which bothered me somewhat.

Martha had an assistant who was an attractive lady in her thirties. On one occasion, I walked in on a conversation about the size of carrots and cucumbers. The two ladies and one of the deliverymen were laughing and giggling. Martha mumbled something about how "the kid won't understand." They were right, because it was much later that I figured out what they thought was so funny.

Upon arriving at that store, grocery list in hand, I would call out the items and Martha would fetch each item and bag it at the counter. In those days, a dollar would fill a grocery bag. The ladies at Martha's would add up the cost and give me the total. This was all done with a lead pencil on scraps of paper. If one did not have enough money, our name would go on the slip and be put in the box and when money became available Martha was the first one to be paid.

While most of our dry goods came from Martha's, we purchased our milk from a farmer named Frenchie who was over the hill—this is a geological expression of terrain, not a reflection on the farmer's age. After big arguments over whose turn it was to go get the milk, my brother or I would hike down there carrying two gallon jugs. Frenchie would fill them for 10 cents a quart. On the way I would pass by cows grazing in the field and they would watch me with wary eyes. The milk was extremely rich—hence mother would pour off the cream and make butter in a churn or save it for whipping cream.

Going downhill with empty jugs was easy, but returning it was all uphill and hard work. Today the farm and pastures are long gone and large housing developments have taken their place. Where the barns and farmhouses stood, now stands a large industrial building that is carved into the side of a once pastoral scene.

There was a second farm near the top of hill owned by a hermit by the name of Dixon. Farmer Dixon lived in a one-room shack located on a knoll that was topographically the highest point on his property. From this vantage point he could oversee most of his land. There was a spectacular view of the Duwamish River valley and all of the industrial might of the Boeing Aircraft factories. To the east, across the valley loomed the Cascade Mountains and to the southeast was the magnificent view of Mt. Rainier. There were natural springs on the property and Old Man Dixon had dammed up the flow into a series of pools that cascaded down the hillside.

Farmer Dixon looked as though he never bathed or shaved so to a little kid he took on an ominous appearance. Always dressed in dirty bib overalls with a patched blue shirt, he wore an old fedora whose crown was stained and the brim of which was no longer stiff, hanging down in loops around the crown. Mr. Dixon looked like a real hermit.

My father's doctor had prescribed goat's milk for a stomach problem that he had and I was sent to farmer Dixon's because he raised goats. At the crudely made gate, a sign posted at eye level stated that Mr. Dixon was a registered farmer of the State of Washington. After knocking on the door, I would wait quite a while for a response. Eventually, there would be some stirring inside and the door would squeak open. There was no plumbing in the little cabin and upon opening the door my nostrils would be invaded by strange odors. "What can I do for you kid?" "Goat's milk," I replied and produced my container. We would go off to the shed where the goats were housed and I would wait while Old Man Dixon did the milking. Goat's milk, like Frenchie's milk, was also 10 cents a quart.

Newspaper Route

At the age of twelve, I was able to get a newspaper route. In those days, getting a paper route was difficult. Your name went on a waiting list and when a vacancy came up, you took it. You had no choice of routes. My route happened to include the hermit, Farmer Dixon. Even though his appearance was always grizzly and fearsome, Dixon was never mean or nasty. There was an incident that occurred at one of Farmer Dixon's pools one hot summer day. Barbara, a neighbor, and some of her girlfriends took advantage of the coolness of one of the pools. They had taken off their clothes and in their nakedness were gaily splashing about when Old Man Dixon came out. He calmly told the girls to put their clothes back on and to please leave his property.

Approaching his cabin to collect for the newspaper, I was always amazed at the array of garden tools hanging all over the outside walls. It appeared that many of them were hand-made. Shovels, rakes, grub hoes and picks all carefully displayed along with a variety of dishpans, which he probably used for bathing and washing his clothing. It was like going to a miniature curio shop. Coils of rope hung neatly along with the garden implements.

There was a wooden rocking chair just outside his door and on nice days one could find Mr. Dixon smoking a pipe and rocking, surveying the valley below. When Dixon was not home, I took the liberty of wandering among his hand-made dams, pools and gardens. Young people are always attracted to water and I was no exception. I was sure there must be some fish in those pools. As much as I looked, however, I never saw one. Looking back, I think about the old hermit's lifestyle and wonder what became of him. It was rumored that he was a veteran of WWI, but I will likely never know. Today, the pools, the cabin and even the knoll where the cabin stood are gone. All flattened and replaced with ticky-tack houses that will never have the character nor the charm of Dixon's farm.

During WWII, the vast, wooded area adjacent to Dixon's farm went through its first transformation. Because the entire hillside overlooked the Duwamish Valley and the Boeing aircraft factory and airfield, it became an important military observation point. A good number of .50 caliber machine gun emplacements were installed along the hillside and there were also barrage balloons placed here. The woods that were once our play area became off limits.

Each Christmas for many years we had cut a fresh tree from these same woods. Many of us kids had read all of Edgar Rice Burroughs's *Tarzan* books. We fantasized about being Tarzan, which led to the building of camps and rope swings all through these woods. Some of the swings swept out over deep ravines and if our parents had only known, I'm sure they would have put a stop to some of our dangerous activity.

Once this wonderful playground belonged to the U.S. Army it became a highly strategic defense position with the gun emplacements and tunnels burrowed deep into the hillside to conceal ammunition stores. The emplacements were heavily reinforced with huge logs and piles of sandbags. The soldiers were housed in barracks that looked like mushrooms pushing up out of the ground. It was quite spectacular when the barrage balloons were deployed. The enormous silver gasbags filled the skies to protect Boeing field as well as across Puget Sound to the Bremerton naval base.

The winds can be fierce at times in the Northwest and when they came up, the balloons had to be brought down and secured. During one sudden windstorm, a balloon broke loose from its moorings and as it lost gas it began to come down a few blocks from our home. With the anchor cables flailing about, the Army was afraid it would short out the electrical power lines. Soldiers finally got it under control and brought it down near the Highland Park Grade School.

In the valley where the Boeing factory and airfield was located, an entire faux city was built on top of the buildings there—pre-fab houses, artificial trees and painted streets that criss-crossed the airfields, all to camouflage and hide the manufacturing plants located underneath. The Highland Park playfield was taken over by the military and four anti-aircraft guns were installed along with barracks and ammunition bunkers, all dug into the ground. Unlike some information I have read, the Army did not take over the school. We continued to attend class daily during the war, walking past the big guns and soldiers on guard duty. At Christmas time the soldiers were invited into the auditorium and listened to the children singing carols. The school also put on Christmas pageants.

Along with the military presence, came a following of "ladies of the night." Of course, at eleven or twelve years of age, we understood nothing about these activities. Raised in a strict conservative home, no one ever spoke about sex. I recall hearing jokes that I didn't understand until years later. During my high school years, I remember the health teacher asking me what muscles would be used if my hands were folded in prayer. This was a typical question in high school health class. Things that are taught in school today are quite different. There were two houses near the army encampments in the neighborhood that attracted a lot of attention. One was a small white house across from ours on 10th Ave, just a block away from the army encampment. The second was located at the top of the hill on 8th Ave. close to the military gun emplacements nearby. This second house became a place of interest to us because of the activity going on there. Our friend, Neil, who lived below this house, observed a redhead often worked in the garden stark naked. Neil also noted that there were others living in the house and they were all parading naked. Well, this was quite exciting news for us, so a plan was devised to somehow get a closer peek. We decided to pretend to be selling subscriptions to the newspaper. Since there were three of us, Neil, my brother and I, we decided the first one would be selling subscriptions to the Seattle Star, then the second one would be selling the P.I. and the third would ask if they wanted to receive the Seattle Times. My brother went first. He knocked, the door opened and to his disappointment, the lady was wearing a bathrobe, but he came back to report that there was a naked babe sitting on the sofa, but she had discreetly covered herself with a newspaper. The lady in the robe declined the subscription, and by the time it was my turn to sell them the Times, the show was over. Those ladies must have had a chuckle over our voyeuristic attempts.

Cougar Hunting with Al Slagel

My friend Don Delong, who I sometimes called by his nickname D.D., had an acquaintance by the name of Al Slagel. Mr. Slagel lived in White Center and he loved to go hunting. He had several hounds that he used for hunting cougar. D.D. was also an outdoorsman and was quite good at hunting and fishing. His stepfather, Vic, was a commercial fisherman who later played an important part in my life.

D.D. called me one day and asked if I would like to go cougar hunting with Mr. Slagel and his friends. I said I'd never been and would like to see what it was all about. I didn't own a rifle, but Don said he would lend me his .22 caliber and he would use his stepfather's 30-06. Every camping adventure we went on seemed to begin in the wee hours of the morning. Long before the sun was up and before any sane person plans to get out of bed, sleeping bags, clothing, rifles, food and ammunition were gathered and made ready to go. The hunt happened during the winter and we were headed into Washington's Glacier Peak area. There would be lots of snow on the ground and weather forecasts predicted snowfall at the elevation we would be hunting, so D.D. reminded me to wear warm clothes and watertight boots.

We arrived at Mr. Slagel's house where we found him already outside packing up his hounds in a trailer attached to his station wagon. Mr. Slagel had a ruddy complexion with a kindly, lined face. Wearing the typical hunting garb of the 1940s—a heavy, checkered black and red mackinaw, wool pants and hat—he was the epitome of a rugged outdoorsman. After double-checking the dogs and kicking the tires, we were off.

We headed north on old Highway 99 to meet up with Mr. Slagel's friend Doc who would join us in the hunt. Doc was retired and lived on a farm in Alderwood with his own pack of hunting hounds. At his house, Doc introduced us to another man, his friend, and their two dogs. With Mr. Slagel's three hounds, we each were in charge of one dog. My dog's name was Yahoodi and he was a very powerfully built hunting hound weighing at least 100 pounds. After the men exchanged a few old hunting anecdotes, the caravan moved forward. It wasn't long before we were in snow country and off the main track and onto an old logging road.

The wilderness in this area is breathtaking in its beauty. As we got deeper into the forest the evergreen trees began to assume different shapes due to nature's pruning with heavy snows. The snow became deeper and we moved until we could go no further on the abandoned logging road.

The first day was spent making camp. We put up a tent, assembled the cots and sleeping bags and readied the lanterns and stove, bringing in food for that evening only. By the time we were done, it was dark and so we made the evening meal of beans with lots of ham thrown in. We were all hungry after making camp. Everything tasted great. After supper the bottle was brought out and passed between adults. The stories of previous hunts began and D.D. and I listened with awe as tales of great successes filled the tent. The flickering lantern deepened the shadows on the speaker's faces, giving the storytellers an unreal and magic appearance. Don and I listened attentively and watched the gesturing of the great hunters. We learned that Doc and Mr. Slagel had hunted cougar all over Washington State, especially east of the mountains where cougars had been taking down many deer and farmers' livestock. The game department decided to even things up and allowed cougar hunting, providing a $50 bounty as an incentive. We also learned that in Eastern Washington it was a lot easier to spot a cougar because of the sparseness of vegetation.

The hunting hound is a fearless and relentless hunter and Mr. Slagel related an episode in Eastern Washington where his hounds trapped a cougar on a barren rock area. Yahoodi charged the cougar and the cat laid him open with a swat, tearing a large square of flesh over his ribs that dangled like a red blanket. This did not stop the dog from attacking, and only seemed to infuriate him further as he stepped up the pursuit. The hunters arrived in time to save the dog. Mr. Slagel pulled the flap of flesh up and around the dog with bandages. The dog took off as if nothing had happened.

Mr. Slagel said that the hounds are always ahead of the hunters and if the hunters don't get there in time, a cougar could kill the dogs. The hunters can tell by the various sounds that the hounds make when a cougar's scent is found or when a cat is cornered.

The bottle was passed many times and as the evening wore on, the stories were embellished with a glaze matched only by the glaze in the hunter's eyes. There were small cats, medium-sized cats and so on, and like fish stories, the cats kept getting bigger and bigger. Finally it was time to turn in and plans were made for the next morning. Mr. Slagel, D.D. and I would start the hunt and Doc and his friend would go out later. I had the feeling that Doc had consumed more than his share of the bottle and needed to sleep in.

D.D. and I, being anxious to revel in this new experience were up earlier than Mr. Slagel and the others, so we went out to tramp around in the snow. Across the valley we could see majestic Glacier Peak covered in snow and with the rising sun peaking out from the cloud cover the rays of light were striking the mountain casting it in a glorious pink color. As I stood mesmerized by the beauty, a huge avalanche suddenly cascaded down the side of the mountain into the valleys below. It was a spectacular sight and I remember it vividly. The sound of it came across the valley, delayed by what seemed like minutes, but what was probably only a few seconds. I ran back to the tent to report the event. I theorized then that the early morning sun had weakened spots in the snow enough to make the avalanche happen. After a breakfast of coffee, eggs and bacon, we made our final preparations. Today, whenever I smell the aroma of coffee outdoors, like Pavlov's dog salivating at the dinner bell, my mind falls back to every hunt, fishing trip or camping I participated in.

All bundled up with our rifles in hand and dogs on leash we hiked off to begin looking for cougar tracks in the snow. It's not hard to find them and the dogs seem to know if they are old or fresh. They will follow an old track, but without the excitement that a fresh track will create. After what seemed like hours of plodding through the snow we finally came across fresh tracks. I'll never forget what happened in the next few seconds. Yahoodi lunged forward so powerfully that he jerked me right off of my feet. As I weighed only about 30 pounds more than the now bounding hound, I hung on for dear life while he crashed through the snow, dropping the rifle so I could hang on to the leash with both hands. I could see D.D. behind me, picking up the rifle while I was being dragged until I finally had to let go. I brushed myself off and when D.D. and Mr. Slagel caught up, he told D.D. to let the other dog go to follow Yahoodi on the hot trail and he kept his dog and instructed us to follow the howling, whooping dogs. He said not to worry, the dogs will eventually come back to camp.

Don and I trudged on and I soon learned why we were recruited for this hunt—we were young enough that we might keep up with the hounds. The snow was up to our knees then and was waist-deep in places. While the dogs leapt through the snow like it wasn't there, Don and I struggled to stay within hearing distance of their howling. Periodically, we would catch up to the dogs when they had lost the scent. Mr. Slagel had told us that cougars are very smart and when tracked will start to circle. They have the capability of leaping up to twenty-five feet and will do so, sideways from their old track, to form an ever-widening circle. The hounds come to the point where the cougar has left its track via lateral leap. At this point the dogs are busy trying to pick up the scent, giving the cougar a bigger lead.

Another trick that cougars do, according to Mr. Slagel, is to jump from tree to tree in the thick forest canopies of Western Washington. Our pursuit went on until early evening. You can easily get lost in the forest at night, but as long as there is some light you can usually follow your tracks back out. We finally caught up with the dogs as they were searching for the lost scent. We determined that the cougar had made it up into the thicker forest area and would not be found that day. I got hold of Yahoodi's leash and Don leashed up the other dog and we retraced our steps back to camp.

Doc and his friend had already gone out and come back except for one dog that had gotten off on a deer scent. Doc explained that this sometimes happens with a young hound and it will run itself until it drops or is picked up by a farmer or another hunter. The dogs are tagged so if found a telephone call usually brings the owner to the rescue. Doc was hoping that this would be the case. Night fell and Mr. Slagel did not return. D.D. and I were very worried and around camp that night we fretted. Doc told us not to worry, that Mr. Slagel is an old woodsman and knows how to survive. We became more worried when it began to snow. It snowed all night and in the morning there were several inches of fresh snow. The plan for the day was to gather the hounds and go hunt for Mr. Slagel. We were all ready to set out for the search when a figure appeared out of the snowy dawn preceded by a dog.

We were all much relieved to see it was Mr. Slagel. He said that his dog had gotten onto a scent and by the time he caught up with him, it had gotten dark and had started to snow. He searched the area and found a dead tree snag that was loaded with pitch. He set it on fire in hopes that if we were out looking for him he would be easier to spot. The snag flared up like a giant torch and burned until it toppled over, spanning a small ravine. Mr. Slagel crawled under it, scraped away the snow and with some evergreen limbs, made himself a bed where he and his hound went to sleep. The heat from the smoldering snag and his dog kept him warm and when daybreak came he simply walked back to camp. Though he smelled like a smoked ham, he was alive.

It was Sunday and since it was still snowing, we all sat around the stove in the tent and talked about survival stories and whether or not we should go for another hunt. Not knowing how much longer the snow would fall, we decided to break camp and go home. The snow was deepening on the logging roads and had we stayed another night we might have been snowed in. Cougars are majestic animals with great cunning and courage and while the older hunters, and especially the hounds, were disappointed, I am glad we never saw a cougar and had to shoot it.

Part II • Army Years

The War Years

As the war continued many daily necessities had to be purchased with ration cards. Meat, butter and gasoline were all rationed. Various metals and materials became scarce. To earn extra money we collected rubber tires, scrap aluminum, brass and copper. Toothpaste tubes were made of lead foil so they were also saved to be recycled into bullets. Tin cans were opened at each end, flattened and saved for the war effort. I always wondered about those toothpaste tubes after learning about the dangers of lead poisoning. No one thought about things like that then, but years later, I read about the Roman nobility who died early in life because they drank their water from lead pipes and their wine from goblets of lead.

A diary kept by a woman who had been in the Japanese controlled Santo Tomas Prison Camp in Manila revealed that the Japanese took every bit of scrap metal they could find to feed their war machine. Corrugated metal roofs and siding, bicycles, autos, trucks, stoves were all confiscated, put on ships and sent to Japan. The difference between the Americans and the Japanese was that while they confiscated the materials forcibly from any source available, U.S. citizens were freely giving and collecting whatever was needed for the war effort. It was also unfortunate that the U.S. sold scrap metal to the Japanese up to the day Pearl Harbor was attacked.

The war was played against the background of heroic movies, novels and comic strips here at home. In the movies, the stars performed miraculous acts of heroism. Most of the airplanes that were shot down belonged to the enemy and you never saw anyone actually killed. When an Allied plane was hit, a fade-out was employed or the plane flew off-screen with smoke trailing. The enemy always had the face of evil. Japanese pilots were depicted with evil grins as they gunned or bombed American or Allied troops. All of the comic books portrayed the Japanese, Germans and Italians as horribly evil people. Newspapers were filled with stories of atrocities committed by the enemy. This propaganda certainly had its effects on all of us as we entered high school. The soft young matter of youth is sauce for the master chef. So it was that we called our enemies with the emotion-filled terms "Japs" or "Krauts" and much worse.

It was difficult trying to be a normal happy-go-lucky student when the shadow of war hung over us like the Sword of Damocles. Conversation usually ended up with which branch of service one was going to join. Every one wanted revenge over the evil people we were taught to hate. When Pearl Harbor was bombed it directly affected many families in the Puget Sound area. Some 1500 soldiers and sailors from this area were killed in the surprise attack. A neighbor of ours, Kenneth Brakke, 19 years old, went down with many others on the battleship *Arizona*. He is memorialized on the monument that straddles the sunken ship. The war news and propaganda prepared our minds to fight.

Enlisting U.S. Army

In 1945 I was able to get a job at Frederick and Nelson, the "Nordstrom" in Seattle at the time. My job was to pick up all of the parcels that people had purchased on the various floors and take them to the delivery area for mailing or shipping. I was paid 35 cents an hour, which was better than previous jobs at Kresses Ten Cent Store, where I earned 25 cents an hour. Many things happened in 1945. President Roosevelt died, the war in Germany was over and the war with Japan ended suddenly in August with the atomic bombing of Hiroshima and Nagasaki.

I happened to be working the day the war with Japan ended. In celebration Frederick's gave everyone the day off and I joined the wild crowds in the streets of downtown Seattle. Fourth and Pike was a sea of people and traffic was at a standstill. After four years of war, all the pent up emotion was released in a joyous, raucous celebration. People were shouting, blowing horns and dancing in the streets. There was hugging and kissing amongst total strangers. It was a wonderful moment to experience. I was anxious to get home and share this joy with my parents and brother and sisters.

I was still attending high school when the Japanese surrendered. Many of us were so hyped-up about going into the service that we were disappointed when it all came to an end. After four years of exposure to super patriotism generated through the media, we were mentally prepared to go to battle. Graduation was in 1948. My friend Don Chase and I went to the naval recruiting office to enlist. Don was accepted and I was rejected because of high blood pressure. Don was inducted and was off to boot camp. His parents were upset because I was not accepted. We had planned to be together sailing the seven seas. I went to the Army recruiting office where again I was rejected. At the age of 18, I could not believe this was happening to me. I went to the family doctor, Dr. Malarkey, and he gave me tranquilizers that lowered my blood pressure to where it was acceptable. I passed the physical and was told by the recruiter that I could go to a military school of my choosing.

My first choice was the Army language school at the Presidio in Monterey, California. The Army radio school at Fort Monmouth, New Jersey was choice number two. Our parents taught us the Russian language so I thought this would easily get me into the Presidio. Unfortunately, I did not get my first choice. At the time I enlisted I was out of sequence for the language school, which had a six-month cycle. The day of departure was sad, my family cried. My dad in Russian said to go with God. I never saw him alive again. He died of a heart attack during the April 1949 7.2 earthquake that struck the Seattle area.

My father hated war. He was a graduate of the czar's naval academy and served in the "Great War." He was wounded and then fled to China when the Bolsheviks came to power.

When I was about sixteen, someone had given me a 22 single-shot rifle that needed repairing. I thought it was a great gift and excitedly showed my dad. He was so agitated at the site of the rifle that he grabbed it from my hands and threw it as far as he could into the woods next door. I never understood this act until I saw the wounded in Korea. That night with a flashlight I retrieved the rifle and secretly started to restore it. I made a number of trips to Warshall's, an icon in sporting goods, on First Avenue in Seattle. I spent many hours browsing through the store. My imagination went wild looking at fishing tackle, camping gear, rifles, pistols, maps, charts, packs, sleeping bags and anything that had to do with the outdoors. On the second floor you could buy parts to repair guns. It was like going to a museum. I purchased all the necessary parts and put the rifle back together. To my great disappointment, I could not get the thing to fire. The sales person told me that I could have purchased a new rifle with the money I paid for all the parts. To me, there was something important about repairing this free gift, but

I suppose I should have listened to him. It was a sad day when some years later this store shut its doors forever.

Boot Camp

Arriving in Fort Ord, California on a sunny September day I was checked into Company C to start my basic training. Along with various items of clothing I was issued an M-1 rifle. The rifle and I became very well acquainted and I could assemble it with my eyes closed.

Basic training passed by very quickly. The memories that still linger in my mind about California revolve around the picturesque sleepy town of Monterey. In 1948 this beautiful place hadn't yet been discovered. I watched the sardine boats come and go along Cannery Row. I was fascinated watching pelicans diving into the sea for their meals. A song that was popular at the time was *Bella Bella Marie*. The music seemed to blend with the charms of Monterey and I loved to listen to the refrains of that piece as I wandered about. Palm trees lining the streets and the lazy autumn sun made me feel in concert with the surroundings. (

Monterey Bay

There was an enlisted men's club constructed on the bluffs overlooking the Pacific Ocean. It was called the Million Dollar Club, as that is what it cost to build. Looking out over the ocean you could forget the drills of the day and enjoy the sunsets with fellow recruits sipping a beer.

Our drills consisted of marching, obstacle courses, bivouacs and shooting on the rifle range. We also had to take our turn at kitchen police duty. On one occasion while pulling KP the mess sergeant yelled, "You, you and you are going to peel potatoes. Keep the skins thin and get all the eyes out." The pile of potatoes was enormous and the work progressed slowly. One of the guys noticed a machine and discovered it was an automatic potato peeler. Through a whirling action the spuds bounced around against an abrasive surface removing the skins. Water flushed the residue down a drain. We quickly threw potatoes into the machine and turned it on. We watched them turn into clean white balls. The only problem was that to get all the eyes and imperfections out the machine was run until the potatoes were about the size of ping-pong balls. Of course we completed the job in less than half the time allotted and reported to the mess sergeant. He couldn't believe it until he saw the size of the potatoes and realized what we had done. We were chewed-out and given more potatoes to peel to supplement what was needed to prepare the meal.

The corporals and the drill sergeants were always yelling and screaming, keeping all of the recruits running and hopping. One of the favorite expressions the sergeants used was, "Soldier, if you don't straighten up, you and I are going to the hospital and they will be digging my boot out of your ass." Strange what one remembers about boot camp. On one occasion I asked the corporal if he knew where my friend Jonesy went. The answer, "The last time I saw him he was running down the street between Company C and B with a broomstick sticking out of his ass playing mine sweeper." It was tough getting a straight answer.

The collection of guys in boot camp represented a cross section of American life. We had farmers from the Midwest and milk truck drivers from Oregon, high school grads from the western states and Latinos from California. One in particular I remember, Hernandez. His mother used to send him quarts of pickled green peppers each week and it was something to watch him plop a whole green pepper spiced with jalapenos into his mouth. I asked him how could he eat those things without catching fire. He would say, "It eezzz gooood, you try." I thanked him but declined.

The mixture in boot camp brought together good people as well as the bad. I used to sleep with my wallet under my pillow until someone at night slipped it out from under my pillow without waking me. After that I kept everything locked in my footlocker. The guys from Oregon were friendly and we spent a lot of time together swapping stories at the Million Dollar Club. The milk truck driver was full of stories about his exploits delivering milk. There were probably a lot of unexplained pregnancies along his milk run. I wondered if that was why he enlisted.

Boot camp was suddenly over. The army gave me my second choice of schools, radio repair. Two weeks before completion of basic training I was given orders to pack up and go to Fort Monmouth, New Jersey. The school was known by its acronym, MIT, Monmouth Institute of Technology.

The Troop Train

My orders were presented early so as to fit into the start cycle of radio repair school. I said goodbye to all my friends of Company C. I stood on the railroad platform on a cold rainy December day waiting for the troop train. I thought to myself, if the weather is going to be like this, I am glad to be leaving early.

The train finally arrived. I tossed my duffle bag and boarded the train. To my surprise the train was already packed with troops and I was put into the last car. This turned out to be a blessing. The train had picked up soldiers at various camps from San Diego to Fort Ord. The train now turned to go south. I watched Fort Ord disappear in the misty rain.

We were told not to leave our cars. Each day there was a roll call and head count as the train crawled south toward Needles, California. The blessing of being on the last car was that you could go to the end of the car and stand on an open platform and view the countryside as the coal fired locomotive chugged along.

The climate grew warmer as we neared southern California and soon palm trees came into view. In the town of Needles the temperature was in the 90s. It was a relief to step out on the platform and get some air. The train was not air-conditioned and there were no sleeping accommodations. All the cars were coaches. We had to sleep sitting up. Whenever the train made a stop they would chase us out on the platforms for calisthenics. The train moved slowly with a gentle rocking motion. The rhythm of the rails was hypnotic and it was easy to fall asleep.

We crept up the mountains in Arizona and soon we saw patches of snow. I spent most of my time on the platform watching the beautiful scenery in Arizona and New Mexico. I recall a spectacular sunset over Arizona—all the shades of reds, yellows, blues, lavenders and purples.

Texas was a nightmare, hot, dry and the air stifling. I cannot recall what city we pulled into but we were side tracked in a rail yard with cattle cars all around us. We were there all day in the stifling heat. As is so prevalent in the military, no one seemed to know anything. Everyone wondered how long we would be in the unbearable heat. Chow would come out of a car somewhere ahead in large metal containers and was slopped into our mess kits. After eating, kettles of boiling water came by to dip the mess kits into for cleaning. It is a wonder no one got sick on this trip. Finally, as evening approached, the train slowly started to move out. I swear it took two days to get across Texas, nothing there to see from the train.

Things started to green up again in Louisiana. I remember crossing the Mississippi River. At the point of crossing the river is very wide and the slow moving train took what seemed forever to get across.

I did not realize how segregated things were in the south in 1948. When the train stopped we did our exercises and were told to use the restrooms on the platform. I went into the wrong one. *Colored Only* the sign said, but I only saw the sign *Men*. After a great deal of commotion I was directed to a *White Only* restroom and *White Only* drinking fountains and *White Only* everything else.

Turning north we traveled through the Carolinas, Virginia, Washington D.C., Delaware and on into New Jersey. The trip took a total of seven days and we miraculously survived the food, the lack of sleeping accommodations and what seemed to be an endless ride.

Fort Monmouth

It was December and very cold in New Jersey. Snow was falling and continued for weeks developing into the biggest snowfall in twenty years.

I was assigned to Company X and it certainly lived up to its designation.

Company X, Main Street.

I later learned that these buildings housed Italian prisoners during World War II. The buildings were single storied and the exteriors were covered with black tar paper held in place with slats of wood lath. The black buildings in their white setting presented a depressing site. The gloomy gray skies and falling snow gave the appearance of a scene from the steppes of Russia.

The author

The company commander was an alcoholic and the mess sergeant was a gambler who would steal food from the kitchen and sell it outside the camp to subsidize his gambling habit. Between the company commander and the mess sergeant a gambling den was run nightly in the recreation hall. Every evening the place would be packed with people from all over the fort and also civilians who were let into the camp through the fence. Company X was located on the perimeter of the fort. A residential street abutted this side the full length of the camp.

The first sergeant who ran Company X, Sgt. Zaworsky, seemed to be the only sane person in our enclave. Friday and Saturday nights were exceptionally raucous in the gambling hall. The noise went on until sunrise. I made one or two excursions into the establishment just to see what was going on. There was one dice table and several poker tables.

Through the dense smoke I could see every table filled with players.

One scene that impressed me was the dice table. Arms waved wildly with fists full of money. The shouting was a steady raucous din. Sgt. Cash, the mess sergeant, held the dice and was shouting to cover bets. On the table there was a pyramid of paper money that was at least a foot and half high. Who kept track of the money I could not tell but the shouting and betting went on through the night. I was told that the military was aware of these games and had some undercover people there to watch out for cheating.

The barracks I was housed in was right next to this mini-Las Vegas. One night I was suddenly awakened by a great deal of yelling and shouting coming from the hall. All the lights went out and I could hear people running out. The fellow in the bunk next to me was a gambler and when he came in, panting heavily, I asked him what happened. He said they caught someone cheating who was carefully marking the edge of cards with his fingernail. When discovered he made a dash for the lights and took off. I guess everyone grabbed what he could off the tables and ran out like rats from a sinking ship. Whenever I see the program *Mash* I think some of it was inspired by what went on in Company X.

Our arrival at Fort Monmouth in December of 1948 was a few weeks ahead of the start of the next school session. We had a great deal of spare time. I asked Sgt. Zaworsky if I could get a leave to go home. Christmas was just around the corner and I thought it would be nice to be with family. He said I didn't have enough time in and as much as he would like to give me a leave, he couldn't do it. It was my first Christmas away from home and being in a strange place and not knowing anyone I felt very lonely.

The guys from Philadelphia, New York and New Jersey could go home on their weekend passes. This left the barracks more than half empty. There was a corporal who loved to sneak up on you and put you on duty. You had to be on your toes, rise early, get dressed and just get out of camp. Cpl. English was a large, heavy-set Indian with a very large round reddish race decorated with a thin anchovy mustache. His hair was closely cropped and receding. He would quietly sneak into the barracks and assign anyone lying about to KP, latrine duty, fireman duty or guard duty.

I met a fellow from Washington State and on Christmas Eve we wandered into Red Bank, New Jersey. The snow was deep and we wore our combat boots, woolens, gloves and a heavy wool GI overcoat. We plodded in the snow through the residential district. With a light snow falling we could see lighted Christmas trees in the windows and hear the refrains of carols drifting from various homes. At that moment I had never felt lonelier in my life.

Back in our tarpaper barracks we had two pot-bellied stoves located near the exit doors at each end of the building. The floor was wood so the stoves were set on a brick hearth. They were coal fired and had to be tended continuously. If the fire went out, it was difficult to get it started again. On occasion when the fires did go out the buildings quickly became ice cold. With the weather continually in the teens it was the duty of the fireman to be on watch all night and through the day to keep the fires burning.

One day Cpl. English caught me and I was assigned duty as a fireman. I was stationed in the boiler room near one of the latrines where it was always warm. It was important that hot water was always available. Firemen were issued a coal bucket, a shovel and a scoop. Every couple of hours I made the rounds through all of the barracks and stoked the fires.

81

In my heart I was always a firebug, going back to the age of five or six when our family lived in a house across the street from Woodland Park in Seattle at 5530 Ashworth Avenue. There was a great deal of vacant property nearby covered with wooded vegetation. My sister and I had built a camp in the woods. We stealthily took some matches out of the house. The plan was to build a fire and make some tea. It was the month of August, hot and dry. Experimenting with matches, I set the woods on fire. In a few minutes the entire hillside was ablaze threatening a row of houses at the top of the hill. Fortunately police in a patrol car across the street in lower Woodland Park were watching a basketball game. They immediately called the Fire Department.

My sister and I ran up the hill for home and passed my mother frantically coming down the hill. The police signaled my mother that the Fire Dept. had been called and my sister and I hid in a secret place in the attic where we were immediately discovered. I always wondered how did my mother know exactly where to look? We both got a spanking from my mother and later again from my father when he came home from work. So you see, I was an experienced fireman.

Every two hours I set out with my bucket of coal and shovel to stoke up the pot-bellied stoves. I opened the dampers and got the fires going so intensely that the pot-bellied stoves were glowing red. After a couple of rounds the guys sleeping nearest the stoves were bitching about the heat. I dampened the stoves to reduce the heat.

Life in Company X was unlike the life in modern barracks that had bathing facilities within the same building. In Company X one had to go out into the snow to a separate building to use the toilets and showers. It was necessary to get fully dressed just to relieve oneself. The latrines were set up for use by the Italian POWs. Everything was out in the open, the toilets, showers and urinals. With this arrangement, prisoners could be watched at all times. The only thing that was hot in the latrine was the water. There were no pot-bellied stoves. A trip to the latrine in the middle of winter was very quick. Combat boots worked well to get through the snow.

The chow hall was not much better. The food and the atmosphere could be likened to a prison. With the mess sergeant absconding with the food we seemed to get served a great deal of S.O.S. (shit-on-a-shingle). It was chipped beef cooked in a creamy white sauce and poured over a dry piece of toast. The only good meal I can remember was turkey served on Christmas Day.

Our barracks leader was a staff sergeant named Hodgkins who was attending radio repair school. He was a veteran of WWII and had served in France and Germany. He had a deep loud voice and everyone would snap-to when we heard his booming orders. He was about six feet tall and built very square like a solid block of wood. He had piercing blue eyes and a large scar on the side of his face and his lower jaw was slightly offset from his upper jaw. His head was topped off with a buzz cut.

After I became better acquainted with him, I asked him about his jaw and scar. He said that during the Battle of the Bulge, he and his platoon were sent out on a night patrol. With the Germans quickly advancing, Hodgkins and his men found they were behind the German lines and a firefight ensued. Everyone scattered and ran, hoping to get back to friendly territory. Running through the deep snow was tiring and after 15 to 20 minutes of all out effort, he stopped to catch his breath. Leaning against a tree he gasped for air. Suddenly in the darkness two huge arms came around the tree and a voice from behind was yelling in German. He was captured along with many others and placed in a prison camp.

The Germans did not have much to eat near the war's end. The prisoners got very little or nothing at all. The Allies were eventually able to contain the Bulge and counter attack. The Germans, continually marched Sgt. Hodgkins and other prisoners ahead of the advancing Allies. As they moved they were not being fed. At one point they were marching through an apple orchard and someone must have realized that there were probably apples lying under the snow below the trees. The men broke ranks and started digging with their bare hands through the snow. With a minimal number of guards the Germans did not try to restrain the men. Sgt. Hodgkins said he found an apple that was rotten but he popped the whole thing in his mouth and as he put it, it was the sweetest, most nourishing thing that he had ever experienced.

Finally the Allied POWs were put in a camp far behind the front lines. The daily meal was potato skins cooked in water to make a broth. The German soldiers got the potatoes and the prisoners got the skin. On one occasion standing in the chow line waiting to get his portion of potato skin soup, he looked into his tin after the German ladled the watery broth. He noticed that he didn't get any potato skins. He complained to the German guard standing nearby. "No skins, no potato skins." The guard raised his rifle and with the butt hit him in the jaw and broke it. This also cut the side of his face. The Germans did not do anything medically to help him so it mended over time with an offset. As he explained, that is why the scar and the strange looking jaw.

Smitty and Others

A fellow soldier I befriended was a guy named Smitty. He was from Stanwood in Washington State. Smitty was about six feet tall and had a head of very blond wavy hair. His face was heavily scarred from acne. He spoke very softly and was quick to laugh. He and I chummed around together. One day he came by and told me he had bought a car and invited me to look at it. He was very proud of his purchase and told me he had been looking for this model of car for a long time. It was a 1937 Cord with an electric gearshift that you operated with two fingers. He bought it for $300. We spent a lot of time together cruising Long Branch, Red Bank, Atlantic City and other parts of New Jersey. Smitty said he was going to ship the car back to his hometown and restore it. It was in good running condition and had no serious dents. When we left Fort Monmouth he was sent to a different area. I never did see him again and I have often wondered what he did with the 1937 Cord.

Smitty, Alex and the 1937 Cord

Another fellow I met at Fort Monmouth was Weatherup. He had fallen in love with a New Jersey girl and they were married. Her family had a huge peach orchard and farm. In November of 1949, he and his new in-laws invited Smitty and me to a Thanksgiving dinner. Being away from home, this gesture was very well received. It was very kind of those people to have us share turkey dinner. On other occasions they invited us to dances that were held in that farming community. I was introduced to square dancing. With allemandes right and left, Smitty and I were always going in the wrong direction.

Our barracks in Company X housed a mixed bag of people. We had rebels from Kentucky, Tennessee and Georgia who openly displayed Confederate flags above their bunks. We also had African-Americans, one from Philadelphia named Kennedy and another from the deep South named Mullins. Mullins and I used to workout together at the gymnasium lifting weights. Unknown to me this did not sit well with the rebel crowd and I became a northern Yankee "nigger" lover. Mullins was very powerfully built and the rebs never confronted him directly. There were a lot of back-handed comments ricocheting around the barracks on many occasions. The rebs couldn't stand being quartered under the same roof with Negroes.

One evening a bunch of us went out for pizza. The fellow from Tennessee had too much beer. All the way back to camp he was railing on me, northern Yankee "nigger" lover and other derogatory comments. I calmly tried to tell him that my parents were not in this country when the Civil War started and they left their homeland in great fear of what the communists would do to them. He would not let up and finally said something that triggered my adrenalin. I was bench-pressing 300 pounds at that time and was probably in the best shape of my life. As he swung at me, I grabbed his arm and put it into a hammerlock, threw him to the ground and sat on him. I tried talking some sense into him for at least half an hour. It was well past midnight and the guys in the barracks overhearing our conversation said, "Let him go so we can get some sleep!" He never looked in my direction or spoke to me again.

Cpl. Ernie English was still lurking about looking for volunteers, but with most guys now on to his ways he was hard pressed. He began to snag volunteers as they gathered expectantly for mail call at company headquarters.

Mail call

Before he called out the mail, he would say OK you, you and you, latrine duty, you, you and you KP and so on. We learned to get around this by not going to mail call. Later in the day, when Ernie wasn't around, we picked up our mail from the company clerk.

Sgt. Hodgkins loved to play pinochle. I learned the game and joined in. I had a good partner, Private Tibbets from Texas and soon we could not be beat. The thing about playing cards with Sgt. Hodgkins was that when Cpl. Ernie came looking for people to pull duty, he was reluctant to break up the game with a person that out-ranked him. Tibbets was a typical Texan and loved to brag about Texas. The most far-fetched tale he relayed to us was about how hot the sun got in Texas. It was so hot you could get sunburned through your shirt. He was very serious about this and we all looked at each other and nodded.

I became acquainted with a guy from Philadelphia named Mitch. He was a lady's man and was very clever about avoiding any extra duty. He liked to drink and one day almost did himself in falling asleep in his bunk with a lighted cigarette. New Year's Eve was coming up and he said, "Let's go to New York City to celebrate!" I thought it was a great idea and we were off to Red Bank to catch a train that took us to the ferryboats going to New York. Snow was falling but that did not deter us. We put on our combat boots, woolen dress uniforms and donned our woolen army overcoats.

Mitch said we could get a bottle of whiskey in New York and then go from bar to bar ordering ginger ale for a mixer. He said we had to be careful when pouring the whiskey so the bartenders wouldn't see us. This was done holding the glass under the bar counter. At that point in my life the strongest thing I ever drank was a beer. We purchased a bottle of whiskey at a liquor store and were on our way.

New York, New Year's Eve 1948, we tramped through the snow from bar to bar. On 42nd and Broadway the snow was getting close to knee deep. I can't remember which bars we drifted in and out of but I do remember Jack Dempseys. Midnight came around and we were both on our hands and knees under a bar looking for the cap to the whiskey bottle. Mitch had dropped it while uncorking the bottle.

I didn't think the bartenders cared that we were pouring our own drinks. It was New Year's Eve and New York was celebrating in a giant snowstorm. Thousands of lights made the snowflakes glitter like falling stars. A force of about 100 policemen stood at attention in the middle of the intersection of 42nd and Broadway. I guessed they were there to see that things didn't get out of hand.

It didn't take much whiskey to send a nice glow throughout my body. In wandering and whooping "Happy New Year!" we came across of couple of girls from Brooklyn. After engaging them in conversation they invited us to come to their place. We boarded a subway that the girls had guided us to. The snow seemed deeper in Brooklyn. With high steps we made it to one of the girl's homes.

The mother at the door became hysterical as she greeted us, shouting "You drunken soldiers!" and reprimanding the girls for picking us up. The door slammed in our faces! We were told to leave as only a Brooklynite could say it with an accent barely understandable. Like idiots, we stood staring at each other as the snow swirled about, trying to remember how to get back to the subway station. Stumbling through drifts we suddenly encountered a car plying slowly through the snow. The car stopped and the window cracked open, a nice couple offered us a ride to the station. I have often thought that had those kind people not come by we would probably have frozen to death in the snow. It was about 3 a.m. and there was not a light to be seen anywhere.

On the subway back to NYC, Mitch continued drinking whiskey straight out of the bottle and became very obnoxious and started to insult other passengers on the train. I could not handle him and eventually left. I got off at 42nd and Broadway and tried to figure out how to get back to the ferry to New Jersey.

I walked from 42nd and Broadway all the way to the docks. The snow was knee deep. I followed the elevated rail line, walking beneath it until I reached the docks. I bought a ticket and boarded the ferry. In New Jersey I caught the train to Red Bank. It was somewhere between 7 and 8 a.m. by the time the train pulled in. There was no one about anywhere, New Year's Day and everything buried in white.

I found a small cafe that had just opened and the lady behind the counter looked at me and I at her. Her eyes were red with dark shadows. It was obvious she had partied all night. I must have looked the same to her, she said, "Coffee?" I said, "Yes," and we both sat quietly sipping our coffee. That was my first trip to NYC, but not the last.

Monmouth Institute of Technology

Fort Monmouth was a school where we were to learn radio repair and the Morse code. After the holiday break we were assigned to various school buildings. The simplistic way that the Army organized the subject matter was impressive. We started with electrons and how and why they moved through wires, how batteries worked and the difference between alternating current and direct current. Every piece of radio equipment depended on vacuum tubes. We were taught how a signal moves through a vacuum tube, how the plates and cathodes worked and how the signal was amplified. We learned about capacitors, resistors and transformers. This basic knowledge was applied to radio receivers and transmitters. We then bugged or made inoperable various pieces of equipment so we could troubleshoot them. This went on for several months. At graduation we were given certificates stating that we were qualified radio repairmen.

Quick Trip Home

In April of 1949 there was a 7.2 earthquake in Seattle that caused a great deal of damage. Our group had just marched back from class and everyone was talking about the big quake in Seattle. People were asking me if I had heard anything. I told them I knew nothing about it. After a few days Sgt. Zaworsky called me out from the assembled troops and told me he had bad news for me from home. My father had died. Evidently when the earthquake struck there was a great deal of panic at the Boeing Aircraft Company. Everyone ran for the tunnels for protection. Then when it looked like things were breaking up, everyone turned and ran the other way. My dad had a heart attack and never recovered. Sgt. Zaworsky with the help of the American Red

Cross enabled me to get an emergency leave to go home. Arrangements were made with Northwest Airlines and I got a seat at the very tail of the plane. It was the only seat available. The plane made one stop at Billings, Montana for refueling.

There was a great deal of sadness at home for all of the family. The last time I saw my dad alive was when I was leaving to go into the Army. My brother who had also joined the Army was stationed in Guam and it was not possible to make arrangements to get him home. The Army gave me one week of leave and the time passed very quickly and before I knew it I was heading back to Fort Monmouth by train. The only thing I remember about that trip was changing trains in Chicago where the winds were howling. In New York's Grand Central Station I was approached by a gay man. I denied his advances and ran as fast as I could with my duffle bag and caught a taxi that took me to the ferryboat back to New Jersey.

Many years later, my wife brought up a story about the quake. She was working as an Easter bunny helper at the Frederick & Nelson department store, which traditionally put on a good show at both Christmas and Easter in the window at the corner of 5th and Pine. Kids lined up for a turn to talk to the Easter bunny. There was a door from the sidewalk into this space and the Easter bunny helpers would guide the kids in, seat them on the Easter bunny's lap and take their pictures. As these events were taking place, the earthquake struck. The street was seen as a series of waves moving toward the window. The building shook violently and the large storefront windows waved in and out but did not break. The Easter bunny panicked, jumped up, threw off his enormous head and ran for the door, hitting the door so hard he took the doorknob with him and was last seen headless, running up Fifth Avenue waving the doorknob. Needless to say, he was fired.

Another Trip Home

During the Christmas holiday of 1949, I was able to get a furlough for ten days. The school shut down and I didn't want to hang around the camp for another Christmas. As a buck private there was not much money in my pocket. I had to figure out a way to get home. A fellow GI told me about catching rides on military planes.

From Lakehurst, New Jersey I was able to hitch a ride. This journey turned out to be quite an experience. We had to sign in and wait for a plane heading west. My first hop was from New Jersey to Columbus, Ohio. The airplane was a twin-engine Beechcraft. Being the only passenger I rode in the seat next to the pilot. I felt pretty good, no long wait for the first leg. This feeling didn't last long as the wait in Columbus lasted many hours. I was getting little information from the corporal in charge. He would inform stranded passengers about available flights. I became very impatient and went to the pilot's ready room and started asking which way they were headed. One fellow said he was going all the way to Seattle. I asked if I could go too. He told me to go check out a parachute and meet him next to Hanger B. I grabbed a chute and went by the corporal telling him I had a ride. He was pissed off that I had gone around him. Somehow I had the feeling that I would still be waiting there had I not acted on my own.

The only problem with the flight was that it was taking a very circuitous route to Seattle. Columbus, Ohio to San Angelo, Texas, Texas to Arizona, Arizona to California then on to Seattle. The C47 was a bare bones airplane. No finish inside and you sat on metal bucket seats facing people on the other side. There were seven passengers heading west plus the pilot, copilot and a sergeant who was in charge of the plane.

The flight was uneventful until we approached Texas. The sun had gone down and the sky was dark with heavy clouds. It was there that we ran into a horrendous thunderstorm. Flying at five or six thousand feet in a tin can, the noise was terrifying as we were pelted with hailstones. It was so loud in the aircraft that you had to shout at the top of your lungs to be heard. The pilot's cabin door popped open and the sergeant yelled, "Put on your chutes!" Evidently what was happening is that the head winds were so strong we were getting low on fuel. The plane shook violently as we all struggled to put on our chutes. I thought, "Oh my god, I've never jumped out of an airplane!" It was the first time I'd ever put on a parachute.

Would it open? Fortunately we did not have to jump. We made it to San Angelo, Texas and landed with about ten minutes of fuel left in the tanks. Another aircraft, I believe a B-24, had encountered hailstones as big as baseballs. There was damage to the leading edge of the wing and broken glass. They had landed a few minutes ahead of us. After refueling and dropping off all the other hitchhikers we continued on to Phoenix, Arizona. We were put up overnight in air force barracks.

The next morning the sergeant said I had to help him with the airplane. It turned out to be a simple task, I had to watch that the elevator flaps on the wing moved as the sergeant manipulated the controls. The same went for all the moveable parts in the tail assembly. The pilots arrived and soon we were off to California. We landed at the Northrup aircraft factory and were met by managers of the company. They let us use their executive bathrooms with showers. They then said they wanted to show us something that was in a special hanger. The year was 1949 and we were looking at Northrup's Flying Wing. They said the project was top secret so we felt very special to stand there and view this advancement in air technology.

The sergeant looked at me and said, "You and I are going out to get drunk." I told him I really didn't drink and I was only 19—you had to be 21 to get served. He said, "Don't worry about it," and added that he would see to it that I got a drink. In those days I only shaved about twice a week and there was no way I could pass for 21. We took a cab to a nearby nightclub and sat at the bar. The sergeant ordered two drinks. The bartender said "No." to me and then the sergeant started his yarn about if a guy is old enough to fight for his country he should be able to drink. He went on to say I was going overseas and may never be back so a drink should not be denied. At that point I didn't know if I were going overseas or anywhere beyond Fort Monmouth. The sergeant continued with such convincing veracity that the bartender finally gave in. He winked and said, "See, I told you I'd get you a drink." We didn't get drunk and enjoyed the evening.

The next morning we were off to Seattle, the last leg of what turned out to be a three-day journey. We landed at Boeing Field. I thanked the pilots and sergeant for the ride and caught the Highland Park bus in Georgetown that took me home.

My furlough was shortened by the three-day plane trip and as I had planned to take the train back to the base, which took another three days, this left very little time at home. It seemed like the next day I was on the train heading back east. My mother had fixed me a box of chocolate chip cookies and some fried chicken to snack on. It was a coach car again and the only thing I recall about the trip is Chicago where it was a few degrees above zero and snowing with the wind howling. I had to change trains there and before I knew it I was back in New York and then Fort Monmouth.

The Pentagon

When we finished our training at Fort Monmouth, a number of us were selected to go on to other schools. I was sent to Washington, D.C. to school at the Pentagon. There I would study communication centers, single side band transmission and more about transmitters and receivers.

The only place in the Army where you did not have to salute an officer was the Pentagon. Generals, colonels, majors, captains and lieutenants abounded by the hundreds. If one had to salute, he would be walking about with his hand glued to his forehead.

Architecturally, the Pentagon was an interesting building—five stories tall and five rings deep. The rings were given letters A B C D E and the floors numbers. So if you were looking for room 5A113 you knew it was on the 5th floor in Ring A and room #113. This method of signage made it easy to find your way through the largest office building in the world.

We were stationed at North Post Fort Meyer, located directly across the highway from the Pentagon. There was a tunnel under the highway connecting the two structures. The living quarters at North Post Fort Meyer were like moving into the Ritz-Carlton after our stay at Company X. The buildings were one story in height and we had rooms, each room housed two men.

The Pentagon was a city in itself. It was said that 30,000 people worked there. The transportation system from the city came in under the building and the people coming to work would rise vertically in elevators to their work areas. There was a shopping center at this lower level where you could even buy household appliances. In the center of the Pentagon was a large park area with benches and walks and shade

95

trees. At the kiosk in the center one could buy food and enjoy it in the park. On sunny days I spent a great deal of my lunch hour in this pleasant space.

Interior court at the Pentagon)

The Pentagon had its own sewage disposal system. The sewage was processed and then spread on the government lawns as fertilizer. When the pentagon was constructed, the process of deodorization had not yet been perfected. The odors during hot humid days made it uncomfortable for the olfactory senses.

I had arrived in Washington, D.C. in January of 1950. I was surprised how cold it was. The basin that is surrounded by Japanese cherry trees was solidly frozen over. I took a stroll around this basin on a very cold winter day. The ice covering the basin had melted about a food back from the edge of the embankment. I came across an African-American who was jerking a line with a jig on it along this open strip of water. I stopped and asked what he was doing. "Jigging for fish," he said and showed me a string of fish four to six inches long that he had caught. He said that when the ice starts to melt from the edge of the bank, the fish come into this space to feed. We talked about fishing and I told him about how I had fished in Washington State. He told me he was going to have a nice fish fry when he got home and continued "jigging" for fish.

In the Pentagon our group studied radio transmitters that were located in a building on the grounds of Fort Meyer. These transmitters were enormous. They were fired up every time Air Force 1, the President's plane, was in the air. The space where the transmitters stood was a very large room with high ceilings. The floors were polished so you could almost see your face in them. The place appeared ready for inspection by any President. Whenever the President's plane took to the air, two transmitters were fired up. One was in contact at all times and the second would be on standby in case the other one failed. The vacuum tubes and coils in these units were gigantic. To change a vacuum tube in the transmitter required plumbing skills as well as electrical knowledge. These tubes were water-cooled and were of such a size that they were brought out in a wheelbarrow when exchanged. The guys that were permanently stationed there told me about cooking chicken by holding it attached to a stick inside the transmitter coils. This was long before microwave ovens came into existence. The microwaves from these huge coils cooked the chicken.

Not all of the guys in our barracks were being instructed in radio repair. Some were going to school to study military photography and other technical skills associated with military activity. There is always one screw-up in every company. In our barracks we had a guy that would not bathe, have his uniform cleaned, shine his shoes or polish his brass. He was so filthy that he gave our barracks a black mark during every inspection. The guys got tired of it and one night they hauled him into the shower, took his clothes off, hung him upside down by his feet to the showerhead and scrubbed him down with GI floor brushes and GI floor soap. He turned red all over but he was clean. There was little problem with him after that.

We were sent to Laplatta, Maryland to learn about various antennas and the way signals were sent around the world. The large antennas in use at that time were called rhombic antennas. A great deal of open space surrounded them. This was to insure no interference with the signal. The signal sent by the antenna was bounced off the ionosphere that varied in thickness from daytime to night. Angles of transmission had to be learned and coordinated with frequencies used. If the transmission were powerful enough you could bounce a signal halfway around the world. When the sunspot cycle was active it would thicken the ionosphere and really fowl up the transmission, sometimes completely eliminating it. Today we have satellites and signals can be bounced off them with great accuracy and practically without problems.

Old Friends Meet

My childhood friend Donald Chase had joined the Navy and was stationed at the Norfolk naval base in Virginia, which was a very short train ride from Washington, D.C. Don called me and said, "Let's get together in Washington, D.C." Great idea, and the following weekend we made arrangements to meet. Both Don and I were weightlifters. We decided to go to the YMCA to use the gymnasium. Don had progressed quite rapidly in his lifting and had won the amateur weight lifting title in Virginia in his division.

At the YMCA we met another fellow who worked out with us. He was a handsome man in his twenties with black wavy hair and dark brown eyes. He was about six feet tall and well built. This new acquaintance kept asking us what we planned to do that evening. We told him that we would probably have a hamburger and malt, go to a movie, and then I would take Don to Fort Meyer where there were always plenty of vacant bunks on the weekends.

We finished our workout, showered, dressed and had our hamburger and malt, then went to a movie. Coming out of the theatre we ran into the guy we met at the YMCA. What a coincidence, he offered us a ride in his car and suggested that we stay at his place overnight. We both thought it was a good idea, so we joined our new acquaintance, chatting about weightlifting as we drove to is house.

Later in the evening he started bringing out all sorts of pornographic pictures that did not impress us. Soon he asked if either of us would like to get under the sun lamp. I said I would and was directed to an alcove off the kitchen. After getting some rays the guy comes in and says one of us will have to sleep on the bench that was under the sun lamp and the other would have to sleep with him in his queen-sized bed. At this point Don and I thought everything was on the up and up. I said being that I was already on the bench I would stay put. This turned out to be a wise decision.

In the morning the guy cooks us breakfast, ham and eggs, coffee and toast. Everything was great but Don was not saying a word. After breakfast he asked us what we wanted to do. Don quickly said he had to get back to Norfolk and asked for a ride to the train depot. On the way Don didn't say a word. We said our goodbyes and briefly talked about getting together next weekend. Don left and the guy drove me back to the Fort.

Next weekend Don called and we talked about plans as to what to do. I said, "Let's call up that nice guy we met at the YMCA, he has a car and we could get around better and see a lot of Washington, D.C. The next line from Don was "What, that son-of-a-bitch! He's as queer as a bed bug, I'll explain everything when I see you."

Upon Don's arrival the following story was revealed. Sometime after midnight Don was awakened by a hand creeping up his thigh. Don leaped out of bed and threatened to punch the guy out. He promised he would leave Don alone. An hour passed and Don was again awakened by a hand feeling his leg. Don leaped out of bed, "That's it! I've had it!" The guy begged and pleaded with Don, "Please don't tell your buddy." He said, "I will not touch you again." He was afraid that the two of us would beat the crap out of him. I didn't hear a thing through the night and had a jolly good breakfast as Don sat silent. Needless to say, we never went back to the YMCA and never saw that fellow again. Instead we did the tourist thing in D.C., visited all the monuments and museums.

School was winding up for me and I had finished with scores at the top of my class. Another fellow, Jim Askins, and I were asked if we would like to go to school in Chicago. This would be at the factory where the latest piece of radio equipment was coming off the assembly line. It was called the electronic multiplex and had 365 vacuum tubes

The electronic multiplex

It had the capability of taking a 60-millisecond teletype signal and breaking it down so four messages could be sent simultaneously on one frequency. Jim Askins and I were the first GIs selected to learn how to service and maintain this equipment.

The first installations were to be in Hamburg Germany and Tokyo Japan. We both wanted to go to Germany so the Army let us flip a coin to make this earth-moving decision. As fate would have it, the coin did not turn in my favor and I was going to Japan.

The Chicago School and a New War

The decision as to who went where was made before we left for Chicago. The orders given to us covered our stay at 5th Army Headquarters on Lake Michigan, all the information about the school, a 30-day furlough prior to going to Japan and the method of transport from Seattle to Tokyo. The final sections covered my assignment to the 71st Signal Service Battalion in Tokyo. The packet of documents was about an inch thick outlining the details of what I would be doing for the next year. I had joined the Army for a term of three years. The military sent me to various schools for nearly two years. I was now trained to repair any piece of communication equipment that the Army had in service.

During my 30-day furlough in June of 1950 the North Koreans invaded South Korea. This event would drastically change things for me. My furlough ended and I was on an airplane heading for Fairfield Susin Air Force Base in California. As I mentioned earlier, the plane carrying General Travis had crashed the day before my arrival causing a great deal of confusion. GIs leaving for the Far East were backed up in the terminal. It seemed like I would never get out of there.

Finally I was put on a chartered Northwest airliner and flown right back to Seattle. The airplane was a four-engine prop type. To get to Japan the route was through Alaska. There were several refueling stops, the first being Seattle. So one day after leaving Seattle, I was landing back at the Seattle-Tacoma airport! They said we had several hours layover while the plane was being refueled. I asked if I could go home as my mother's home was close to the airport. They said it was OK, but be sure to be back at 5 p.m. exactly. I called my sister and she picked me up and everyone was surprised to see me again so soon. There was a lot of conversation and goodbyes all over again and I rushed back out to the airport. The plane was readied ahead of time and they were all waiting for the missing passenger. I ran across the field up the ladder and jumped into my seat. All aircraft were boarded on the field.

We landed in Anchorage and the Air Force fed us a steak dinner while they readied the plane for the next leg.

Flying over the Aleutians to our next stop Shemya provided very exciting views of the Aleutian Islands. Airplanes flew at 12,000-14,000 feet making the landscape below quite visible. I remember seeing volcanoes along this chain of islands and some of them were actively smoking. The disadvantage of flying at this altitude is that at times you are flying through clouds. We encountered plenty of thunderheads that shook the plane violently. Dropping down and then suddenly up in jerks made a lot of the guys very sick. The stewardesses were very busy running up and down the aisle handing out lined paper bags that were quickly filled. Looking out the window, I saw bolts of lightning crashing all around us, I was reminded of the C-47 ride to San Angelo, Texas. Again I thought we were done for. The plane pressed on through the storm and eventually we approached Shemya.

The island is in perpetual fog with the wind blowing at some 40 plus knots. I was looking out the window for some signs of land—nothing but fog. Suddenly I could see huge waves crashing against a very rocky shoreline and the end of the runway just behind the rocks.

The airplane was coming at an angle of 30 degrees to the landing strip because of the violent wind. We hit the pavement with a bang and suddenly everything seemed all right. We motored up to the fog-shrouded control tower. Other buildings, barely visible appeared in the thick blowing fog. We were told to go to the mess hall for breakfast. The wind-blown fog had made everything wet including the interiors of the buildings. The GI trays upon which the KPs placed our food felt wet and greasy. The guys stationed there looked a miserable lot. The food was dumped unceremoniously on our trays. The pork sausage links that fell on my tray were so overcooked they broke into pieces, the scrambled eggs cooked to the consistency of cotton balls, the coffee must have been on the stove for weeks. I dumped everything and decided to look around outside.

I wandered off into a landscape that I had never seen or experienced since—grassy dunes with the wind howling. Soon I could not see very far and panic overwhelmed me. I couldn't see the buildings I'd left or anything in front of me. I thought "My god, what a place to get lost!" I retraced my steps in the sand and safely reached the base. The whole setting reminded me of an Alfred Hitchcock film I had seen. I came across some abandoned gun emplacements. I remembered the Japanese had invaded the Aleutians during WWII. I do not know if this is one of the islands that they had occupied. I was momentarily overwhelmed with fear and depression standing in this dark and lonely place.

Back at the mess hall I talked with some of the guys stationed there. They said minimum tour of duty was six months and they could hardly wait to get out. I talked to the pilot who flew us there and he said he had never made a landing without instruments. He said he thought the place was fogged in 365 days a year.

Off to Korea

We took off of the last leg of our journey to Japan. Landing at Haneda Airport in Tokyo we were loaded into trucks and driven to a holding company to await assignment. The place was called Camp Drake, Headquarters of the First Calvary division. I was called into an office to be interviewed by a 2nd lieutenant. I gave him my large stack of orders. He didn't bother to look at them and merely said, "Sorry we are reassigning everyone coming in to the Far East Command." After working miscellaneous duties for three days in the camp my name was called out and I was assigned to an infantry unit going to Korea.

After my knees gained their composure I reflected, this isn't so bad. All of the bitterness and resentment that I was brainwashed with during the war years of the 1940s could now be taken out on the North Koreans.

At 20 years of age it is amazing how you feel indestructible. I was given an M-1 rifle and a blanket, put on a troop train with about 500 guys and on my way to the southern port of Sasebo.

Unlike the modern trains in Japan today, the locomotive was coal fired and steam driven. The passenger cars appeared to be first class. The upholstery was cloth, a rich deep blue color. The woodwork, which decorated most of the interior, appeared to be mahogany and was stained a deep reddish brown. The combination of colors and materials gave the interior royal appearance. It was five years since the war with Japan had ended and the economy was still struggling.

The train slowly worked its way out of Tokyo, and suddenly we were in Yokohama. The two cities were like one contiguous city. It took a long time to get out of the urban areas and into the countryside. Rice fields appeared stretching for miles along both sides of the track. The raised areas between the fields divided the land, giving it an appearance of a giant quilt. The design and colors gave the land an appearance of a giant Mondrian painting. The workers moved among the rice fields and along the raised areas. I saw a lady carrying a large basket on her head steadying it with one hand. In her other arm she was holding a baby that she was nursing. It appeared that WWII had never touched this area. I wondered how a peaceful looking people could have ever participated in such a violent conflict.

The farms gave way to cities—Nagoya, Kyoto, Osaka—and then more farms and more cities—Hiroshima, Fukuoka and finally the port city of Sasebo. In the harbor there were many warships, British and American. Looking at the British warships, it appeared discipline was lacking. You could see laundry hanging all over the place. There were also a many very noticeable areas of rust. By comparison the American ships were spic-and-span. It reminded me that my dad also didn't think much of

105

the appearance of the British Navy. The harbor of Sasebo is beautiful, hills rising from the sea dotted with houses poking out through lush green vegetation.

Cruise to Pusan

In the harbor a troop ship waited to transport us across the Sea of Japan to Pusan Korea. The war was not going well for the Allies and the North Koreans quickly advanced to within 50 miles of Pusan. The Allies were fighting for survival. This small bit of land held by the Allies became known as the battle of the Pusan Perimeter. There was a lack of supplies for the GIs. At the beginning of this sudden war the blanket I was issued was my sleeping bag. The M-1 rifle was my weapon. Everyone else had 30 caliber carbines with banana clips. Soldiers were collected from all over the Far East Command and loaded on the Japanese cruise liner. The military had contracted with the Japanese for transporting troops. The officers got the first class cabins and the troops the second and third class passage areas which turned out to be large open areas on the lower decks with wall-to-wall tatami mats. You planted yourself in any open spot available.

Gambling ran rampant. I don't know what it is about heading for battle, but it seems to bring out cards and dice in great numbers. It's like what the heck, I may not be coming back so let the cards and dice roll to see how lucky I am. It reminded me of the days at Company X at Fort Monmouth, there were huge mounds of paper money everywhere with guys rolling dice and playing cards. I did not know a soul on the ship as I was thrown in with a unit that I had not trained with. It turned out to be a very lonely trip. Conversations were very short without any real meaning or depth. It felt as though something ominous was going to happen. I felt that no one wanted to get acquainted. Let's have a good time while we can and roll the dice.

Pusan

The harbor of Pusan was crowded with ships loaded with men and materials. This was the only major harbor that was available to the Allies in 1950. The North Koreans had driven the Allies south into a small area of land at the top of the Korean peninsula at the widest point.

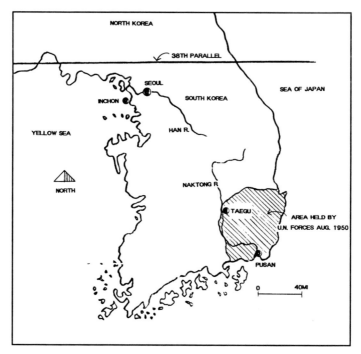

Battle of the Pusan Perimeter

The land was about 100 miles wide and fifty miles deep. The city of Taegu was just behind the front line. This was General Walker's Headquarters. We soon learned that we were headed there. We boarded another train very unlike the train in Japan. The locomotive was steaming and ready to leave. The Army had given us several cans of C-rations to eat enroute. We were not fed on the ship so everyone was hungry.

In Pusan there were thousands of Korean refugees that were fleeing from the North Koreans. They milled about like cattle on the streets and in the train depot. The influx of this mass exodus created a shortage of food and housing. I don't know where those people stayed at night, but during the day they were all in the streets. Everywhere you looked was a sea of bobbing heads.

I opened a can of C-rations that according to the label contained chicken and vegetables. I looked at the contents and to my dismay sitting on the top of everything was a large green pepper. I hated green peppers and without thinking, as the train was pulling out of the depot, I threw the can with its contents out the window. This was a big mistake. There was a roar from the milling crowd and as I looked back it was like a scene from Africa when the wildebeests stampede. In the month of August it is very hot in Korea. A cloud of dust rose as the people fought over that small can of food. I did not realize that these refugees had probably traveled for miles without food. I did not feel good about what I had thoughtlessly done. Each time I think of Korea that is one of the scenes that come to mind.

On to Taegu

The train slowly pulled out of Pusan and we were heading north. It was very hot so every window on the train was open. As we chugged along the card and dice games resumed and there was a great deal of joking and laughter. I had to go to the bathroom and I asked the sergeant in charge of our car where the head was. He pointed toward the end of the car. I opened the door, which opened into a tiny compartment and did not see anything that looked like a toilet. I returned to tell the sergeant there was no toilet. He barked, "Look around, you'll find it." I returned, opened the door and scrutinized everything very carefully. My eyes came upon a round brass ring in the floor and I could see the railroad ties rushing by below. I figured this must be it. But when you have to go squatting, trying to hit the hole in a train that was rocking up and down and side to side, was an extreme challenge of marksmanship. I braced myself with both hands to the sides of the compartment and did my best. I looked around for TP, none anywhere. Fortunately I had a GI handkerchief that sufficed. I dropped it into the brass hole and it quickly disappeared. I went back to my seat and said nothing to the sergeant.

The train moved through rolling hill country that was barren of trees. There were not many farms in this naked landscape. I was told the Japanese had been in Korea for forty years and stripped the land of its mineral and timber wealth.

The train slowed down and we were approaching some kind of junction. It was a small town on the way to Taegu, which is now called Daegu. Here we came upon a scene that I will never forget. I can only liken it to the scene in the movie *Gone with the Wind* when Scarlet went to fetch the doctor at the railroad station. The scene in this little junction was similar—wounded soldiers all over the place on the ground, on flatbed cars, some lying on their backs, some sitting, some standing. All were covered with white bandages that were red with blood. It was a Korean unit that had taken a severe beating when hit by the North Koreans. The wounded had just been brought back from the battle and were awaiting treatment for their wounds.

It was like someone had pulled a black curtain over our train. The mood changed from the boisterous dice and card games to the reality of what we may be facing. The train grew quiet as everyone picked up his weapon and started to clean it, going through the motions to confirm that the rifles were in working order. No more laughter, no more joking, no more games. The train moved on to its destination.

We were approaching Taegu through a tunnel. The train stopped and we were told that the train would stay in the tunnel until nightfall. Someone said that the city had been shelled and they did not want to expose a trainload of troops in the daylight hours. Night fell and the train slowly pulled out of the tunnel and slipped into the depot.

The city was blacked out. The train stopped next to a loading platform. There were about 300 of us milling around in the darkness. You could not make out the face of the guy standing next to you.

New Assignment

By divine providence an announcement was made. "Is there anyone here that knows anything about communications?" I shouted that I did. I was assigned to a portable communication equipment center in General Walker's Headquarters command post. The rest of the men went to the front to fight the war in the trenches. I often wondered how many of them made it back home.

The city of Taegu was surrounded by mountains and along the ridges of these mountains a fierce battle was raging day and night. During the evening meal we would each be given a ration of two cans of beer. After eating chow we would find a spot to sit on the hillside. We sipped our beer while watching P-51 Mustangs, which were used early in Korea before jets, drop loads of Napalm along the front lines—somebody was really catching hell up there! There was a fierce battle up on Saddle

Ridge, one of the ridges surrounding the city. Looking at the exploding Napalm was spectacular. Here we were, out of harm's way watching what looked like a fireworks display. It was very strange to be viewing the war from this perspective—feeling guilty and at the same time fortunate that we were not up there on those ridges. By some miracle on the platform I was called apart and was now viewing the war like a giant picture show. There were human beings dying along those ridges. Deep inside I was glad not to be up there with them.

The women in villages surrounding Taegu would wash our fatigues in the river for a few won. I think that if I had a magnifying glass I would have found Korea crawling with fleas. Everyone was bitten from head to toe and always scratching. We slept in a shelter on the floor. I had not been issued a sleeping bag so sleeping on the floor with my GI blanket was not very comfortable. I thought of the guys on the line and fell asleep battling the fleas.

One day scrounging about in the village I found a discarded woven straw mat. Great, I'll put that under the blanket and perhaps I'll be more comfortable. Big mistake, the thing was not only infested with fleas but in the middle of the night I was awakened by something severely biting me on the back. I reached over my shoulder and grabbed something hard that filled my hand. It was under my tank top, I crushed it in my hand, whipped off the shirt and shook it. Never did find out what this hard beetle-like creature was. The woven straw mat was thrown out and the next morning all my fatigues and undies went to the ladies at the creek doing laundry. It's a wonder any of our clothes held together as the women used stones to beat the dirt out.

One day after viewing my flea-bitten body I asked if there were any place to take a shower. Yes, there was a 50-gallon drum rigged up for bathing. No hot water, but what a relief it was to stand under the cascading water hoping all the fleas would wash off and drown.

The communication center where I worked consisted of three trucks, one housed the communication center, one a receiver station and the third a transmitter. I was assigned to the receiver truck and my job consisted of tuning in the various frequencies the Army was using to get their messages from GHQ in Tokyo. If the equipment broke down I was to repair it. The entire communication center was run by generators which also had to be maintained. One morning we were awakened by the sound of heavy artillery. It sounded very close. We ran out to see what was going on. It turned out to be an ROK unit doing artillery practice on the hill behind us. We were all relieved that it was not the North Koreans breaking through. General Walker's Headquarters were eventually moved to Pusan. It was feared the post might be overrun. This happened after I returned to Japan. I was told that this was the closest a command post had been to the front lines.

Meanwhile, in Tokyo the electronic multiplex on the top floor of the Dai-ichi Building was waiting for the arrival of a much-needed operator. The military in charge sent out feelers to find me. After two years of training in electronics I was sitting in a truck tuning a radio receiver.

Back to Japan

It was some time in September that the Army located me and ordered me back to Tokyo. Pusan was about 50 miles from Taegu. I was to be driven to Pusan in a Jeep. I loaded my duffle bag and rifle onto the back seat and we were off. The unpaved road was graveled and bumpy, weaving through farmlands and rice fields in a low-lying valley surrounded by rolling hills. My driver was a kid from Oklahoma who spoke with a southern drawl. He told me he liked to go hunting for wild game. Every time he saw a crow he would stop and shoot at it. He encouraged me to try it. I aimed my M-1 rifle at a crow perched in a tree, pulled the trigger and missed. This was the only thing I ever shot at in Korea. The crow took off and Oklahoma said, "Hand me your rifle." He took the M-1 and shot the crow in flight. It fluttered down into a rice field. A Korean farmer ran over and gathered it up. I speculated that they were eating crow that evening.

We continued our jolting ride to Pusan. Oklahoma suddenly jammed on the brakes and shouted, "See that! Look over there! It's a pheasant!" I strained my eyes but could not see it. He grabbed his carbine, took aim and shot it through the eye. He ran over and picked up the bird and brought it back to the Jeep. I was amazed at his marksmanship and questioned him about it. He said, "I didn't want to ruin the meat. I'll have the mess sergeant fix it for dinner tonight."

We arrived in Pusan in the gathering dusk of evening. I was quartered in a holding company. I believe the building was a school that had been converted for military use. It was painted a deep reddish brown. The quarters were much better than Taegu—we had cots.

I had to wait for the review of my orders. I wandered around amongst the constantly milling refugees in Pusan. The GIs were taller than the Koreans and you could see their heads bobbing up and down among the sea of Korean citizens. Suddenly I came across a Korean giant. I know he was at least 7 feet tall and towered over all the GIs and Koreans. I had always pictured people of the Oriental race to be of short stature.

Back at the school building, I had to relieve myself and found a bathroom. It was a hole cut into a wooden plank that was not very comfortable to sit on. However it was much better than its counterpart on the train.

113

As I sat minding my business I was suddenly hit with a rush of cold air against my bare bottom. This air was accompanied by a horrible smell. I leaped off the plank and peered into the hole where now I could see daylight. About three stories down I saw a man shoveling the human waste into wooden buckets. The long shaft was like a chimney and when the door was opened far below the cold air and smell rushed upward. I said to myself nothing goes to waste here. They used the human feces to fertilize their rice paddies.

Three days passed and I was called in to see a lieutenant who was reviewing my papers. I saluted him. He looked up and returned my salute. He said, "Minimum tour of duty in Korea is six months, you haven't been here long enough, you're going backup to the front. Get your things together and be ready to leave." The term snafu came to mind.

That evening I was throwing my duffle bag onto a troop carrier revving its engine. Suddenly I heard my name being shouted. Divine providence once again intervened. Back in the office I was given new orders, personally signed by General Walker ordering me back to Tokyo.

The next day I was on a troopship heading west across the Sea of Japan with two other GIs. One was a kid 15 or 16 years old who had lied about his age to get into the Army. He was in the 24th Infantry Division that had really taken a mauling from the North Koreans and he was terrified. He declared his real age and they were sending him back home.

The other guy was older but there was something about him that wasn't altogether. We did some target practice off the stern of the ship. The Japanese seamen threw boxes overboard and we shot at them. With the M-1 I literally blew a box out of the water and it shot up into the air about three feet. The Japanese seamen were thrilled and wanted to shoot. I gave them the M-1 and they took turns. The odd GI emptied his carbine and then threw his rifle overboard. He mumbled something and then went to his cabin. The trip back to Japan was quite different from our trip to Korea. The three of us had the entire ship to ourselves and we could bunk anywhere.

In Sasebo we boarded a train for Tokyo. Soon the rails were carrying us back in the opposite direction we had traveled a few months earlier. We had a two-hour layover in Osaka. The three of us went into town, found a tavern and I had my first taste of Japanese Sapporo beeroo.

GHQ Tokyo

In Tokyo I was assigned to the 71st Signal Service Battalion which was part of MacArthur's GHQ. We were quartered in a building formerly occupied by the Japanese Imperial Marines. The building was located in an area called Roopongi

Main Street of Roonpongi

115

The camp was known as Hardy Barracks. The Japanese Imperial Marines were hand picked soldiers dedicated to protect the Emperor. The barracks were designed to accommodate the height of the soldiers—they had to be at least 6 feet tall. It worked great for us, as we did not have to duck going through doorways.

Main entrance of Hardy Barracks

The structure was made of masonry and covered with white stucco. The building was three stories high and arranged around two courtyards. Every one had a window that looked into the courtyard or out over the city.

Interior court of Hardy Barracks

On the roof of the building there was a Japanese siren from WWII.

Japanese siren from WWII

There was a very spacious day room, an auditorium, a non-com's mess hall, and a GI mess hall. Japanese civilians performed KP duty and in the non-com mess Japanese girls were employed as waitresses. Once a week we had what was a white collar inspection of the barracks. This was to prove we had exchanged our sheets and pillow cases for clean bedding from the supply sargeant.

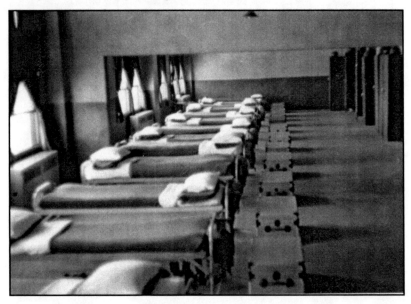

White collar inspection

The life for a GI in Japan was a life of leisure. During the Occupation the 24th Infantry Division and the 1st Calvary Division lived luxuriously with no thought of war on their minds. Many lived off post with their Japanese girl friends. When the Korean War broke out they were yanked out of their mid-summer night's dream and thrown into the front lines of Korea. There was very little advance training and they were given light armament to face the Russian-built T-34 tanks. It was easy to understand why our losses were so heavy and the Allied forces pushed back so quickly. The North Koreans were trained and well equipped.

The Imperial Marine Barracks were very solidly built and from their appearance suffered no damage during the bombings by American planes during WWII. On the roof there was a wonderful view of Mt. Fuji and looking toward the city center you could see the Japanese Diet buildings that housed the government of Japan. You could also see some of the Imperial Palace.

General MacArthur had taken over the Dai-ichi building for his headquarters.

General MacArthur's Headquarters, The Dai-ichi Building

The building formerly housed an insurance company and was the tallest building in Tokyo, 10 stories. It fronted on one of the main streets in the heart of Tokyo. Directly across the street was the Imperial Palace, which was surrounded by a large moat. Between the moat and the palace were the parade grounds. Across the street was Hibiya Park, a luscious green space in downtown Tokyo.

Hibiya Park

A little further up the street were Frank Lloyd Wright's Imperial Hotel and the Ernie Pyle Theatre where Bob Hope came to entertain the troops.

One day several hundred troops were gathered to watch a film depicting the Hiroshima and Nagasaki atomic bombings. The movies were in vivid color showing the victim's skinless bodies with quivering flesh. I will never forget the horror depicted in these films. The military leaders wanted the GIs to see the devastation of atomic war and the suffering it can cause to civilization. Anyone viewing this film would immediately call for a ban on atomic weapons.

Looking north from the top of the Dai-ichi Building was the Union Club where pilots and stewardesses stayed for a rest stop. The electronic multiplex was housed on the roof of the Dai-ichi Building. General MacArthur's office, the cryptograph section and other military offices occupied the rest of the building. From the roof we had a panoramic view of the city.

Moat and grounds of The Imperial Palace

The Diet Building

the Nippon Theater in downtown Tokyo

View of Tokyo in 1950

This spectacular view would cause voyeuristic problems in the future, which I will explain later. General MacArthur was quartered at the

American Embassy on the road to Hardy Barracks. Whenever the general was chauffeured to the Dai-ichi Building the Japanese police stopped all of the traffic from the Embassy to Headquarters. Mac drove uninterrupted, his five-star flags mounted on the front bumper fluttering in the breeze. Japanese citizens lined the streets all the way up to the steps of the Headquarters Building to wave as he passed by.

General MacArthur was highly revered by the Japanese people. As WWII came to a close the Japanese military and government had led their people to believe that the occupying armies would rape and pillage the country and torture the people. The imperial leaders of Japan convinced the citizenry that they would have to fight to the death to protect their homeland. This was a great concern to our military leaders.

How quickly the Japanese minds changed when the atomic bombs were dropped. After the fighting ended MacArthur arrived at Haneda Airport in an unarmed C-47 cargo plane. He stepped out on the tarmac in his khaki uniform wearing his soft floppy hat. He was unarmed. This impressed the Japanese entourage there to greet him and also the Japanese people. He was not the monster portrayed by the leaders of Japan. I believe this is one of the reasons he was revered by the Japanese people. MacArthur was looked upon as a very brave soldier.

In 1951, a friend of mine, Corporal Niprikas, sent General MacArthur a Christmas card. To his surprise, General MacArthur sent him a card in return, personally signed, saying he appreciated hearing from soldiers in his command.

The American embassy and our communication center were connected by UHF transmitters and receivers. UHF stands for ultra high frequency and was a direct line of sight communication system. When General MacArthur's command was taken away from him by President Truman, we did something we were told never to do. We could monitor the UHF transmissions at the communication center on their way to the overseas transmitters. We listened to the personal conversations between people at the Embassy and various people in Washington, D.C. It has been a long time since that took place and unfortunately I cannot remember details of the conversations. There were many expressions of sorrow and sadness in the dialogue. The entire military command and the Japanese people were in a state of shock at MacArthur's removal. Rumors flew about wildly. It was being said that he was removed because he wanted to nuke the Chinese as they massed to cross the Yalu River in North Korea. Another rumor was that he wanted to bomb the dams on the Yalu to disrupt the Chinese advance. Military transmissions to the Pentagon and President that came through our center were heavily coded so we did not know the details of what went on. We sent all transmissions to the cryptographic section for decoding.

General Ridgeway was appointed to take charge of the Far East Command. He came directly from duty in Korea. When he mounted the stairs to enter the Dai-ichi Building he was dressed in battle gear wearing fatigues, a bandolier of grenades and an M-1 rifle slung over his shoulder. This was not a welcome scene to the Japanese people and consequently there were never any crowds to watch him come and go.

I had a friend in the cryptographic section that told me the following. When MacArthur asked Truman for permission to send U.S. troops to Korea he waited in the decoding area to get the message first hand. When the authorization came through, Mac said, "Now we'll show the bastards." The 24th Infantry Division was sent totally unprepared and was brutally mauled by the North Koreans. They fought valiantly a delaying action and reformed at a battle line called the Pusan Perimeter.

The Dai-ichi Building was a very modern structure. It was faced with stone that appeared to be a black polished marble or granite. On the lower floors there was a restaurant and snack bar. The place was always crowded with the top brass of the military. Being the first electronic multiplex technician in Tokyo, I was assigned to the day shift. During these hours the center was loaded with officers that kept us continually on our toes. There were also American civilian employees. The routine was—get up in morning, shave, shower, breakfast, jump into the Jeep for a quick ride to the Communication Center, then back to Hardy Barracks in the evening. The military hired many Japanese civilians to alleviate the unemployment that plagued Japan. Our Japanese driver had a great deal of difficulty shifting gears so we always had a jerky ride with grinding gears.

My job was to keep the multiplex operational. This meant that everything had to be fine-tuned so the signal would be sharp. We could monitor the signal on an oscilloscope before it went into the multiplex for clean sharp edges. On occasion we would be bothered by the sunspot activity and would have to keep changing frequencies until the transmission was clear.

As more multiplex men came into the Far East Command, we were able to organize our duties into three shifts—daytime, evening and graveyard. The Captain left it up to us to decide shift positions. We organized our time to work three days and take three days off and then rotate the shifts. I preferred the graveyard shift because there were no officers and the mood was relaxed. If there were no problems with the equipment I could catnap. This left daytime for playtime and there was much to see and do in Japan.

In Meiji Park there was a large pool built for the Olympic Games, which were never held there because Japan went to war. During the summer we spent a great deal of time at the pool. We met three American girls and cavorted with them in the pool. They were the daughters of married officers stationed at Grant Heights. This made it somewhat difficult to get acquainted with these girls. The oldest girl, Bunny, was about 24, Barbara and Betty about 17 or 18. I liked Bunny but it was Barbara who was attracted to me. She was tall with blond hair and wide face with eyes set wide apart, a nice figure and very buxom. Bunny was well tanned with brown hair and sharp features, but she thought I was too young for her. She was an organizer and put together an aqua folly in which we all participated. Betty was short with blond hair and a freckled face. Calvin was dating Betty and she became pregnant. They decided to get married. It was the first wedding I had attended. Betty was well camouflaged in her wedding dress. Barbara gave up on me and took off with Calhoun. I was left empty handed. Summer passed and I soon forgot about the girls.

Piano Break

As I had lot of time with nothing creative to do, I decided to do something to improve myself. At Hardy Barracks there was a dayroom with a piano. I had the urge to take piano lessons. Through the manager of recreation I was introduced to a Japanese lady who gave lessons. Her name was Toko Fukui and she was a classical pianist. Her husband was a violinist. They lived in the outskirts of Tokyo. I had to take a train to get to their home—riding in a Japanese commuter train is something of an extraordinary experience.

Getting on was easy, getting off was difficult. Listening carefully for the name of the station where I would disembark was at first difficult. Voices announcing the same station sounded different. At each stop more people got on than off and soon I found myself standing in the middle of the car like a stalk in the midst of a tightly bound bunch of asparagus. I listened carefully as the stations were called out. At the station before my stop I would begin to fight my way to the door. Each time I made it off just before the doors slammed shut. Conductors on the platforms at each station would physically shove people into the cars. In the summertime it was rather uncomfortable but in winter it was cozy.

Arriving at the Fukui home there was a ceremony—taking the shoes off, putting on the slippers, bowing and exchanging greetings before sitting down at the piano for lessons. Being inside a traditional Japanese home and taking part in customs that I found most enjoyable opened my eyes to a different way of life. After lessons we would have tea and conversation. Toko had two boys about the ages of four and five. I took lessons for six months and practiced daily in the Hardy Barracks dayroom. Before I was sent back to the states I went for my last lesson and thanked Toko for what she had done for me. I never did become a classical pianist but exposure to the Japanese lifestyle was wonderful.

The Night Shift

Midnight to 8 a.m. turned out to be a most interesting experience. Don Moser worked this shift with me. Don worked on the relay equipment. He was about 5'9" tall with a receding hairline. His nose curved outward reminding me of Greek noses. The hair that remained was black. His head was olive shaped set with brown eyes that shifted quickly as he spoke, his body animated with movement and gestures. He would greet you with a quick smile and a laugh. He was married when he joined the Army but that did not slow his amorous inclinations. Sometimes he let his mustache grow into a thin anchovy shape. When all the equipment was operating properly we sat around and relaxed.

One evening Don found a pair of binoculars left by the day officer. He picked them up and started scanning the night scene around Tokyo. Being the tallest building you could look down into the surrounding buildings. Suddenly we heard a whoop from Don as he gazed into the windows of the Union Club. As I mentioned earlier, pilots and stewardesses were housed there during layovers. The action was amazing as the men and women went at each other. There was no air conditioning in the older buildings and the windows were wide open, with the lights on there was nothing left to the imagination. Don peered into every building surrounding the Dai-ichi. The Bachelor Officer's Quarters came into view—all kinds of action was going on there. I do not know how those guys sneaked the women into the BOQ past the desk and guards.

From that day on it was a race to get to the binoculars. Eventually everybody brought his own. The trouble is nobody wanted to work. From the moment we arrived for duty Don would go missing—out on the roof getting a better view. Don became totally possessed with voyeurism. Long before all of this night action came into view I had purchased a 600-power telescope to study astronomy. The guys talked me into bringing it to work and setting it up on the roof where they lined up for a peek. I could have charged money for a five-minute look.

Somehow word of this night show circulated down to the cryptographic section. Soon the roof was crawling with people who should have been working. It must have made the offices below short-handed. The word eventually got to those in charge and our night show came to a close. No binoculars were allowed to be taken to work.

Don's term of enlistment ended before mine and he was sent home to

Daly City, California. When I was discharged I came through the port of San Francisco. Don and his wife invited me to visit. At his home in Daly City I noticed a pair of binoculars sitting on the table next to the living room window. I said, "Don, is this what I think it is?" Before he could answer his wife Sue said, "Yes, I can't keep him away from the windows, he is constantly spying on all the neighbors." In the army Don worked on IBM equipment. After leaving the military he went to work for IBM. Later he opened his own shop where he bought, repaired and sold IBM equipment and became extremely wealthy.

The Manipulator

In every army there seems to be a guy who manipulates the system. The fellow in our company was Corporal Sorrels. He reminds me of the character played by Segal in the film *King Rat*. He even looked a bit like Segal. Sorrels was about 5'6" with wavy hair that was almost blond. He had a rugged handsome face marked with a few scars. Between his bright blue eyes was a convex nose. He had been a gunner in a B-29 that was shot down during WWII. He parachuted safely to earth and was captured by the Japanese. Wounded by shrapnel he was quick to point out where pieces were still lodged in his body. The Japanese guards beat him and made him bow each time they passed by. As he bowed he spewed forth a volume of curse words. The guards thought they were being honored. During his imprisonment Sorrels learned to speak Japanese.

The black market flourished for years after the big war ended. Many items were scarce. A carton of Lucky Strike cigarettes with the big red dot brought 1,500 yen. The Japanese liked the red dot label. The exchange rate was 360 yen to the dollar and you could buy a carton of cigarettes for one dollar at the PX. The Army knew what was going on. Ration cards were issued and you could only buy two cartons a month.

I did not smoke and always had spare money to buy cigarettes. At the end of the month most of the guys were broke. I would collect their cards and buy several cartons of cigarettes. Most of the GIs had their laundry and cleaning done by Japanese cleaners that surrounded the base. It was at these laundries that the exchange was made. The cigarettes would be placed in the bottom of the laundry bag and covered with clothing, on top were the dirtiest shorts. When opening the bag for inspection the guard would give it a cursory glance and wave you on.

Japanese laundry in Roopongi

Corporal Sorrels was into bigger game. He had watches, booze and new cars. By the time I met him he had amassed enough money to buy a house off post where he spent most of his time. He invited a bunch of us to a party at his place. There must have been a hundred cases of vodka, whiskey and gin stacked floor to ceiling.

When we were on duty together at the Dai-ichi Building we would take coffee breaks in the snack shop. In the elevator he would be confronted by officers of all ranks. They asked, "Hey Sorrels, when's my Buick going to be here?" or "When's my Chevy coming in?" He was importing cars and selling them to the officers.

One night Sorrels got so drunk he forgot where he parked his car and thought it was stolen. He reported it to the MPs. The next day he sobered up and remembered where he had parked. He took a taxi to his car. While driving to his house, the MPs, not being notified that he found his car, stopped him, made him open up his trunk which was loaded with contraband—cases of watches, booze, etc. He was court martialled and busted to private. He told the captain he didn't give a damn because more money would pass through his hands in one year than the captain would earn in a lifetime. He was very cocky and outspoken. With his bravado and talent for marketing he made many friends in the upper ranks. He literally got away with murder. One night he was very drunk. While driving his car he hit and killed a rickshaw driver. It was noted as an accident and he was never prosecuted.

Sorrels discovered that I had a talent for drawing. The officers on my shift had me drawing various radio circuit details. He asked me to draw plans of sailboats. He would have them built in Japanese ship yards and send them to the U.S. The corporal had an entrepreneurial skill. He saw a very cheap labor market that he could take advantage of.

Japan was deep in recession. There were thousands of discharged military people looking for work. The war factories had shut down putting many in the streets. I recall observing a street repair crew working on a chuckhole. It was a cobblestone street. They were removing the loose stones and resetting them. They had chisels and sledgehammers. There were about six in the crew. One held a chisel and another would strike it with the sledge.

Many of the unemployed pulled rickshaws. There were hundreds of them on the streets. The rickshaw was the best way of getting around Tokyo at a reasonable fare. Some of the Japanese had taken up driving taxis. The cabs were 1930s vintage cars that were converted to charcoal fueled burners during the war due to fuel shortages. The burner was a large furnace-like contraption mounted on a platform attached to the rear bumper of the car. Periodically the driver had to stop, run to the rear of the vehicle to stoke the furnace with charcoal. During the winter it was very pleasant riding in the back seat as the warmth of the furnace came through to keep you toasty warm. In the summertime it was pure hell. You could not lean back. One had to sit as far forward on the edge of the seat and hang on to the seat in front to keep from being rocked back on the hot seat as the taxi jerked forward.

Back to Sorrels, I told him that my expertise in drafting was architectural and not naval and the only architectural drawing that I had accomplished was at the high school level. He said, "Don't worry about it. Go to the library and get books on naval architecture and we will build boats."

The war was still going in Korea and Truman had extended all enlistments for one year. Suddenly my three-year enlistment turned into four years. I didn't pick up on Sorrels' offer but we still remained friends. He had gone so far as to contact some wealthy Japanese businessmen to get his boat-building plan started. We did have meetings that I attended. All of the conversations were in Japanese with a great deal of sake being served. It appeared that he had everyone in agreement. I don't know if he pursued his project to fruition as my one-year extension turned into nine months and I was transferred to Camp Drake to await shipment back to the USA.

The Golfer

Don Langteau and I worked together on the night shift and we became good friends. We still exchange Christmas cards. Don Langteau was about 5'8" with a slight build. He always kept his hair in a bristling crew cut, his face was a little wider at the jaw. He had a wide mouth that turned down slightly at the corners giving him a serious look. But when he smiled everything turned up in the proper direction. He had brown eyes that would flash when excited. Don was clean-cut and kept his space in neat order.

Before making the rank of staff sergeant I bunked next to Don in the dormitory. He was a golfer and spent all of his spare time practicing. I knew nothing about the game and he continually asked me to play golf with him. I didn't know how good he really was until much later. He was always telling me he shot par and under which meant nothing to me. We both had a great deal of furlough time accumulated and he talked me into going on R&R to a resort known as Karuizawa. It is a spa about 90 miles northwest of Tokyo in the mountains. There is a live volcano near there named Mt. Asama. We made arrangements through Special Services to spend a couple of weeks there. Karuizawa had a beautiful golf course nestled among softly rolling landscape dotted with pine trees.

Mampei Hotel at Karuizawa

Golf Clubhouse

We were housed in a beautiful old Japanese resort hotel surrounded by gardens, waterfalls and pools. The war never touched this place and once you melded into the setting you never knew there was a war going on. All of the rooms, spaces and gardens were of excellent proportions. In 2000 years of construction the Japanese perfected design and proportion. It truly was a place you could let your mind rest and meditate.

Don Langteau

The author

Don, on the other hand, was anxious to show me the game of golf. The day after we arrived we were on the course joined by two other GIs. The first hole was 220 yards and Don said he was going to use a 2-iron, saying I would have to use one of the drivers to get the distance. He offered to go first. He pedantically went through many details of how to address the ball, where the feet should be, never take your eyes off the ball, etc, etc. After a couple of practice swings he hit the ball and made a hole-in-one. I thought to myself, this is a simple game, you just hit the ball and it goes in the hole. As the day wore on I found the game was more difficult than the experience of the first hole.

As we walked the course Don told me about all the tournaments he had won and sometimes hitting a hole-in-one while playing. I learned about eagles, birdies, slices, hooks and bogies. Don stayed with me on every shot. He told me what club to use, how to hold it and how to hit the ball. I even learned how to put backspin on the ball. The first day I ever played golf I ended up with a 96. Don's name was put on a plaque in the clubhouse for the hole-in-one with three of us as witness. After fifty plus years I wonder if it's still there.

As you play through the course there is a wonderful view of Mt. Asama, the live smoking volcano. The next day Don and I played again. We were joined by a colonel to form a threesome. As the game moved along I landed in a sand trap at the side of a green. Don came over and told me exactly what to do with the nine iron. He said, "Don't hit the ball, you've got to hit behind it taking some sand with it. Don't hit it too hard." I listened to every word. The colonel was holding the pin and I took my stroke. Bounce, bounce went the ball and dropped into the cup. The colonel was amazed and asked how long I had been playing golf. I told him, "I just started yesterday." He never spoke to me again. After years of golf I figured he probably thought I was a smart-ass enlisted man.

Don later played in the Far East Golf Tournament. He was a corporal at the time. The tournament included military from Hawaii, the Philippines, Taiwan, Korea, Guam and all of Japan. Don was the lowest ranking man to play. The players ranked from generals on down. Don won the tournament and was awarded a four-foot tall trophy that the captain at the 71st Signal Service Battalion wanted him to leave with the battalion. He said no and shipped it home. The officers were really impressed with his ability and told him that they would see that he received a golf scholarship to a university in the States. He never did take advantage of this and never turned professional. Ben Hogan was his idol, they were about the same physical size.

Mt. Asama

As we played golf daily, Mt. Asama seemed to be beckoning. We decided to take a day off and see if we could climb the mountain. From a distance we thought the gently sloping sides could easily be conquered by motorcycles that were available for a few yen per day.

The next day we rented two motorbikes and were off. In 1951 the Japanese were not making world-class motorcycles. At best they were oversized bicycles with motors attached. Early on we got an inkling of problems ahead. Trying to negotiate the foothills we found the bikes were gutless. You had to get off and push as the hills steepened. We did reach the base of Asama and looked up. There was not any way these bikes were even going to start the climb unless we pushed them by hand.

Dejected we headed back to Karuizawa. On the way Don's bike throttle handle failed. Upon investigation we discovered that the only thing that held the throttle cable in place was a little ball of solder swaged to the end of the cable. The solder was gone so the cable pulled right through the fork on the throttle handle. There was not enough slack to make a knot.

We came upon a small village in the country and found a blacksmith. He was dressed in the heavy hemp-like garb of country folk and wearing wooden clogs. The dialect spoken in the country was nothing like the Japanese we learned in the city. We finally resorted to sign language, lots of motions, pointing and Don struggling with words, adding an A to the end of American words—bika, cablea, broka, as if that would help. We finally came to an understanding. The soldering iron was heated in a stone furnace with a foot-operated bellows that projected from one side. The blacksmith did not leave the iron in the fire long enough to get hot. So each time he tried to make a solder joint he failed. Don took over, shoved the iron back into the furnace and pumped the bellows until the iron came out glowing red. We finally got a solder ball to hold and were able to drive back to Karuizawa. We gave the blacksmith some money that he refused. We thanked him and we were on our way.

The next day we discovered a local bus that could take us near the base of the mountain. We checked the schedule and early the next morning we were on the bus along with many farmers carrying various fruits of their labors including chickens. Again not a soul spoke English and we could not communicate with the little Japanese we knew. After saying "Mt. Asama" several times the driver finally understood we wanted to get off at the base of the mountain.

Don and I had never climbed a mountain and we came totally unprepared without food, water or any other article that a person undertaking such an adventure would normally bring. We did wear our combat boots and fatigues. At the base of the mountain there was a sign with a Jolly Roger on it staring at us with words in English—"Off Limits." Ignoring the sign we started up. Many Japanese have climbed the mountain so the trail was obvious. This was an active volcano so the ash deposited on the trail was very deep. It was like two steps up and one back as you sunk into the pumice.

The trail up Mt. Asama

Fortunately for us the sun was behind clouds, otherwise we would have never made it. We did reach the summit exhausted and very thirsty. We ran into a group of six Japanese girls who had easily made the climb.

The Japanese girls we met

All of us on top of the mountain. Don is in back and I am sitting on the right

The girls saw our plight and offered us some of the fruit that they had brought. One girl gave me what looked like an apple. It may have been a pear apple. When I bit into it the juice poured out and ran through my fingers. It was the tastiest bit of fruit that I had ever eaten and it immediately quenched my thirst.

The top of the mountain was strewn with enormous boulders that had been tossed out by recent eruptions, many larger than an automobile.

Don on top of the mountain

The author

The sulfuric fumes billowed out of the enormous crater so we stayed upwind. Looking down into the yawning mouth you could see the lava as it boiled and sputtered making sounds like firecrackers popping.

The edge of the crater

I took a number of photos and tried to converse with the girls. Every time we said something they would just laugh. We thanked them in our limited Japanese for sharing their fruit. The return trek was easy, taking large steps and digging our heels into the deep pumice. We wore out the sides of the combat boots in the abrasive ash. A year after returning to the United States I read in the paper that Mt. Asama had erupted sending billowing clouds of ash thousands of feet into the air.

We spent the rest of our time playing golf, reading, writing letters and in the evening watching movies in a small theatre that had been set up in the lobby. Eventually we had to leave this beautiful Japanese garden and head back to our base where duties awaited us in the headquarters building.

Back at GHQ

With the schedule we had organized, three days on and three days off, we had a great deal of time to visit the sites around Tokyo. There were many clubs in the city where you could spend an evening drinking beer and being entertained by Japanese girls that always seemed to be plentiful and available. At 21 I had very little facial hair. I would get by without shaving for two or three days. With rosy cheeks and no facial hair it was easy to convince the girls that I was a cherry boy. This would get you a freebee.

Another friend, Roy, who had a boyish face, would also play the same game. My friend Roy was about six feet tall topped off with a thick mantle of light brown hair. He was slim with a narrow handsome face with sharp features. His face was smooth and clean-shaven.

We visited several clubs throughout Tokyo. One evening we met a couple of girls with whom we danced and conversed. As the evening wore on they invited us to come to their place. After a brief taxi ride we arrived at a very pleasant wooden house with floors covered with tatami mats and a little hibachi stove in the center of the main room. We drank more beer and frolicked about. The girls convinced us that we should be bathed before going to bed. A large wooden tub with very hot water was prepared and the girls helped us out of our uniforms and into the tub. They got in with brushes in hand and proceeded to scrub us down. It was a very delightful experience. It was the first time I was ever in a tub with a woman and gently being washed from head to foot.

After the bath we were carefully dried off and went to bed. The tatami mat floor was the bed with a heavy comforter. The Japanese women were trained to quickly move out from under you just as you were starting to attain a climax. I was amazed at the dexterity and quickness of how this maneuver was achieved.

May Day Riot

Next day I was up before daybreak. Roy wanted to stay and hang out for the rest of the day. It was May 1, 1952. I dressed and left before anyone else was up. There were no taxis around at that time of the morning so I decided to walk back to base. There was not a soul to be seen anywhere. I walked through Meiji Park and was amazed to see all the red flags and banners strung about on every pole and even in the trees. These were Communist banners and flags. I was not aware that these symbols were to signify a Communist rally that was to start in the park that day. Later this demonstration turned into the famous Tokyo May Day Riots.

I walked back to Roopongi without experiencing any disturbance. The parades started later in the day and by mid-afternoon had turned into full-scale riots. It was not safe for any GI to be seen on the streets. I was going on duty that evening and our Jeep driver had to take a very circuitous route to the Dai-ichi Building to avoid the mobs. We left very early, as we didn't know how long it would take to make the trip. We arrived without incident but everywhere cars were turned over and some on fire. Piles of tires were heaped up and set afire. There was debris everywhere.

From the top of the Dai-ichi Building we could see that a huge mob had formed on the Imperial Palace parade grounds. They were preparing to storm across the sacred bridge leading to the gates of the Imperial Palace. The bridge was constructed over the inner moat that surrounded the main palace buildings. There was a large contingent of Japanese police blocking their way. The police carried no guns. They were armed with clubs and shields. The mob was armed with long bamboo sticks with nails attached to the ends resembling a lance. The crowd was shouting and yelling gathering courage to charge the police lines.

Instead, the police charged the mob. The parade grounds were graveled and the whole scene disappeared in a giant cloud of dust. Thousands of people were running everywhere. The police had difficulty fending off the lance-like spears with their shields. Soon the mob was dispersed and running in all directions. Viewing this scene from ten stories up was horrifying. Japanese police surrounded the Dai-ichi Building and as the mob scattered some of them tried to run up the stairs to the entrance. The clubs of the Japanese police went into action. The sound that reached our ears was that of a baseball bat popping a watermelon. Two unfortunate American sailors were tossed into the moat across the street from our building. The riot passed and there was much news about it in the military paper and radio. For several days everyone walked on eggshells throughout Tokyo.

A Night in Tokyo

Late one night Roy and I were carousing in Tokyo. There was a curfew, all GIs had to be off the streets by midnight. On this particular night we either had too much Japanese beer or forgot what time it was. We were walking along a very narrow and dimly lit cobblestone street. Everything was closed for the night.

A second story window suddenly popped open and several girls were beckoning us to come in. The front door was locked for the night and we couldn't get in. I got Roy standing up on my shoulders where he could reach the window. The girls were pulling him up by his arms when suddenly a Jeep with MPs came whipping out of the darkness. Roy jumped down and we both took off running. We ran down a narrow alleyway and jumped over a fence scaring the wits out of a mamasan who was emptying a bucket of water. The idea was to backtrack along the fence while the MPs chased us down the alley. We were stealthily making our way along the fence until we came to an opening where the MPs were calmly waiting for us. They asked, "Why did you guys run?" We really didn't have a good answer. They said, "get in the Jeep and we'll take you back to your base." We told them we were quartered at Hardy Barracks where they dropped us off at the main gate. They said, "Next time don't run, we'll just bring you back to camp." We thanked them and turned in.

Heidelberg Restaurant

There were many Germans residing in Tokyo. Most of them had been there through the entire WWII. Since the Germans and Japanese were allies, these people had the freedom to do whatever they wanted. Some had established businesses in Japan. Near Hardy Barracks there was a restaurant called The Heidelberg.

I wandered in one day soon after it opened and found a it delightful place to eat. The bartender was Japanese and his wife was German. The bartender was a short stocky man with a very round face topped off with thick black hair showing a few white streaks. Under his nose was a thick black mustache. He spoke English slowly with a heavy accent. I sat down at the bar and had a drink and a menu listing various German dishes was given to me. I ordered the sauerbraten and struck up a conversation with the bartender.

He told me he had been trained as a geologist at schools in Germany where he met his wife. She did the cooking for the restaurant. When Japan invaded Korea, China and Manchuria he was sent by the Japanese government to explore those countries for mineral resources that the Japanese needed for their war machine. He and his wife were sent to Manchuria. His explorations opened 132 mines for the Japanese government. These mines contained various metals and minerals.

Everything was good for them as long as the Japanese were winning. They had first-class accommodations at the expense of the government. He and his wife had two daughters both of whom were very beautiful. The combining of the Caucasian race with the Oriental race has produced some very attractive people. I finished my meal and we continued to talk and drink. Being that the restaurant opened recently, it had not yet been discovered. I was their only customer.

He went on about the mines and his work in Asia. As the tides of war changed, they had to leave Manchuria in haste. Their greatest fear came when the Russians entered the war. Russian troops quickly moved through Manchuria. They feared their daughters would be raped by the Russians. The mother made the daughters put on the filthiest rags they could find and put splotches of mud on their faces. The mother gave instructions to the girls, whenever the Russian soldiers came by they were to sit and pretend they were picking ticks and fleas out of each other's hair.

This ploy worked and the girls were not touched. They put their belongings on carts and were able to make it to a port city where they made passage to Japan. He and his wife scraped everything they had together and built The Heidelberg Restaurant. As the evening wore on I was introduced to his wife. She spoke English with a heavy German accent. She was short, robust, outgoing and friendly. Her hair was graying and her spectacles sat on the end of her nose. The conversation continued with the three of us and before long they insisted I meet their daughters. Their apartment was above the restaurant and the mother called the girls down.

Aiko is standing on the left.

I fell in love with Aiko immediately. She was the older sister. Her face was a combination of Oriental and European features set in a frame of long flowing black hair. The nose was European. She had round eyes that were dark brown. Aiko worked in an office located near the main train station in Tokyo.

I was nearing the end of my extended enlistment so we tried to spend as much time together as possible. Aiko showed me places I had not visited. We took picnic trips by train to Lake Hakone, a beautiful area near Mt. Fujiyama. We walked through forests and some of the great temples of Japan. The term of extension was suddenly cut short. I was sent to Camp Drake for processing prior to being sent back to the States. I snuck out of the camp one night and hopped on a bus to Tokyo to see Aiko for the last time. Sadly, I thought of her for years after, but nothing came of it.

Venereal Disease

The American GIs ran amok in Japan chasing Japanese girls. Unfortunately most of the short-lived love affairs were with prostitutes. There was a time that everyone in our dormitory except Don Langteau and I had some sort of venereal disease. The office where you picked up your passes was well stocked with condoms but apparently never used.

There was a guy we called Frenchie. No one was able to pronounce his French name, Suchomeu. The closest they came was calling him Satchmo. Frenchie was short in stature with very round face, topped off with brown curly hair. He had a bulbous nose, brown eyes and a dark olive complexion. His eyes appeared to be bugging out their sockets. Frenchie liked to drink and when he was out on pass he would roll with any female he could find. He would get so drunk that he would have sex in the street. One day he came in with his eyes rolling and his uniform covered with mud and dirt. As I talked to him I tried to get his eyes to focus on mine. They rolled like gutter balls in a bowling alley. I asked, "Where the hell have you been?" As he swayed about he told me he had laid a woman in the street gutter. With his appearance he did not have to convince me further.

Unfortunately he came down with some sort of venereal disease that the doctors could not diagnose. He broke out with sores over his entire body and at night he itched so badly he would scratch himself bloody.

He had to change his sheets daily. He checked out books at the library on sexually transmitted diseases. He read aloud descriptions of some of the most horrible symptoms of venereal diseases that you could possible imagine that originated in the South Seas. There were graphic pictures along with the descriptions. If ever there were a reason to give up sex with prostitutes, Satchmo was the epitome.

GIs could buy booze for a dollar a fifth. They even had 2-for-1 nights. Satchmo's locker was filled from top to bottom with cases of miniatures. It was fortunate that we never had locker inspections. After falling ill he gave up drinking and started reading the Bible. Thinking back on his disease, I believe he was infected with some rare form of herpes.

A bunch of us that served together were shipped home at the same time. We all had to go through a short-arm inspection. Gene, a friend of mine from New York came down with a case of gonorrhea. If it were discovered he would be put in the hospital and have to wait for recovery before they shipped him out. I asked him what he was going to do. He said he would hold his thumb over the blister and hope they wouldn't notice. Once he got on the ship he said he would turn himself in to the Navy doctors. He did get through the inspection. He was married before shipping out and didn't want to return with a blistered weenie.

The troop ship *USS Mann* was a very slow boat. It took twelve days to get to San Francisco. After going through more physical exams I was honorably discharged July 5, 1952. I visited with my friend Don Moser in Daly City and then returned to Seattle and White Center.

Part III • 1952 and beyond…

The Football Team

Coming back from Korea in 1952, a bunch of guys from White Center got together and decided to form a semi-pro football team. I think this was all put together after a few beers at the Happy Hour Tavern in West Seattle. The only two members of the team that I remember are Marv Nelson Jr. and Del Wickline. We got a coach and started our practice at Hiawatha Playfield next to West Seattle High School. A few of the rag-tag team of players had played football somewhere in the past. I remember one fellow claimed he used to be an all-Army end. Through some sort of accident, he was left with only one eye.

After each practice we ended up at the Happy Hour and discussed a name for the team. I do not remember how we came up with the name, but we all decided upon The West Seattle Independents. All of us had jobs so it really limited our practice sessions. I was working on a commercial fishing boat at the time and was lucky to get in town for the games. With the few practice sessions I had, it was decided I should just be a defensive lineman and knock people down.

There were a number of semi-pro teams coming together at the time. A schedule was put together and for our first game we were to play the Bremerton Yellow Jackets, a Navy team. There was the Seattle Ramblers, and another team from Kent whose name I have forgotten, as well as an Army team, the Fort Worden Warriors who hailed from

Port Townsend.

One problem was that we did not have any money so our uniforms were anything but uniform. The game at Fort Worden was a big Saturday night event and the whole town turned out along with many people from the fort. The stadium was well lit and when we came on the field the Fort Worden people called us back into the dressing room. They said we couldn't go out on the field looking like we did, so they lent us their practice uniforms. After they walloped us 38 to 18, they must have felt even sorrier for us because they told us to keep the uniforms. We lost every game we played but the fun and camaraderie made it a wonderful experience for all of us.

The First Job

After getting out of the Army, I wandered around looking for a job. The war in Korea was still going on and the draft was picking off friends of mine that had not served. One of them who had not yet been drafted was Don Delong. He and I were the same age and used to do a lot of trout fishing in streams and lakes throughout the Northwest. On a few occasions we hunted cougar in the Cascade Mountains.

His stepfather, Vic Carlsen, owned a commercial fishing boat named *Loyal*. The boat was kept in the fresh water moorage of the Salmon Bay waterway in Ballard. The dock belonged to a fishermen's supply warehouse and was very close to the entrance of Hiram Chittenden Locks.

Loyal was 50 feet long and carried a crew of nine during the purse seining season and a crew of four when it went to sea as a trawler.

The boat *Loyal* rigged for trawling, Esperanza Inlet. Watercolor by the author

It wasn't easy to get on as a crewmember in those days. You had to know someone and it was especially difficult for a greenhorn. The crew consisted of the captain, cook, a man to pile the lead line, a man to pile the cork line, two men in the skiff to set the lead (pronounced leed) net, pull it up, then come back to the boat to help purse the seine and then come aboard to neatly stack the net. The men in the lead boat also served as spotters looking for signs of fish. It was the duty of every man to look for fish.

George Bernard Shaw had many comments about the English language. I would have loved to hear his comments about the word "lead" which has several totally different meanings, especially on the fishing boat where we have the lead line which has lead weights and the lead line which is a line that is set first.

There were a total of five men working to pile the main body of the seine and Don told me that this was where the greenhorns usually started. The fruit of everyone's endeavors was divided up in shares.

153

Each crewman got one share of the catch, the boat got one share, the net one share, and the boat owner one share. The money derived from the sale of fish for the entire season was divided into shares. First the expenses of the trip were subtracted from the total before the division of shares was made. Don's father, being the skipper, a crewman and the boat owner got three shares, but there was a great deal of upkeep required for the boat and for the boat's net. In the end, the summer fishing season put about $2000 in my pocket.

In the off-season the net was stored in a tall storage loft where each strip of net was carefully hung. About two weeks prior to the start of the season the nets were assembled and the boat prepared. Each six-foot strip of net was sewn together and loaded onto the boat.

In good years, fortunes were made very quickly seining in the waters of Alaska, through the San Juan Islands and in Puget Sound. Don talked his stepfather into letting me join the crew. Because piling the net was the easiest job, most of the older guys were doing that and Don and I were assigned to duty in the skiff setting the lead net. It was simple enough, but very hard work. If the lead line was caught in a fast-moving tide, it took all your strength to pull the net into the boat. Don preferred to be in the skiff because it was fun to run the craft around when we weren't actively fishing. It had a V8 engine and as bulky as it was, it could really move out at speeds up to twenty knots. Don's Dad admonished us many times for racing around. If we had wrecked the skiff, fishing would be over for the entire crew.

These were the days prior to dedicated drum seiners and the main net had to be pulled in by hand over the stern with the help of a power roller that was run by a power take-off from the main engine.

The average water temperature in the summer is 53 degrees and 45 degrees in the winter. When the fishing is good, about 30 boats can be seen at the salmon banks. The summer weather in the San Juan Islands is usually warm and sunny. I cannot remember a trip when it rained for the entire season.

Pursing the net was done by pulling in the purse line, which was at the bottom of the net and was threaded through large brass rings, with the power winch. At the bottom was the lead line, so called because of the lead weights attached to the lowermost part of the net. The brass rings were also attached to the lead line. All parts of the net had to be carefully stacked so that when a set is made, with the boat going at top speed, nothing would snare or snag and cause damage to the expensive net.

During a normal set, the main net was pulled into the boat over the stern with each man handling one strip of net. One man piled the cork line and another piled the lead line. The net had to be piled evenly so that when it came time to feed it back out it would not tear, as this would cause fish to be lost. The evenly piled net flew off the stern with the boat going at full speed. Uneven piling would cause part of the net to leave before the adjoining strips producing uneven stress and tearing the net.

The net was always set in a wide arc. After schools of fish are spotted, usually finning just below the surface, they would encounter the net and dive to try to get under it. The net was designed so that near the bottom it curved back upward. The fish encountering this curve would then swim back up. Don and I would pick up the lead line and work furiously to pull it in, and then we sped back to the main boat.

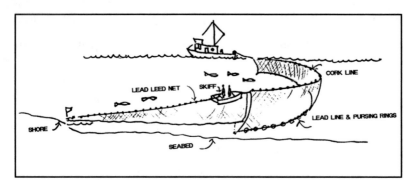

Setting the seine

The lead net is tapered so at the very end it is only about 12" in width. The taper allowed us to toss the buoyed end as close to shore as possible. As the net plays out and follows the slope of the seabed, the fish close to shore would follow the wall of lead net into the larger purse seine. The fishing boat returns to the junction of the lead net and the purse seine, closing the circle. The skiff men hand off the line at the end of the seine and the pursing begins.

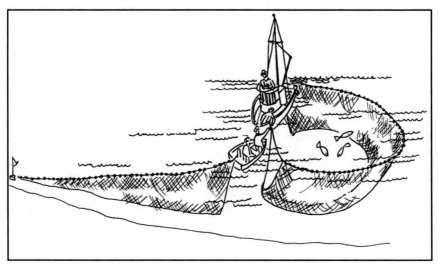

Handing off the seine

There are a few people on the boat that made a lasting impression on me. The skipper, Vic, was a big man with a square, weathered Norwegian face. He had bright blue eyes, wide shoulders and hands so large that when he folded them into fists they looked like two boulders. With a deep, rasping voice he boomed out orders from top of the wheelhouse. Vic had been fishing since he was thirteen years old, and at the time I met him, he was in his fifties. Because of all his years of squinting in the bright sunlight looking for fish, Vic had developed a skin cancer under one eye. The Marine Hospital removed it for him and in the process, removed the wrinkles under that one eye. Vic joked with me that he wished he had gotten cancer under both eyes so they could take out all the wrinkles and have matching eyes. It might seem that Vic was vain about his appearance but this was not so. His ragged craggy face lined with wrinkles gave him the appearance of a man who had been at sea all his life. In places the lines moved upward giving his face a happy look.

Don told me a story about an incident with Vic at the dinner table at home. It was discovered by his parents that Don had had a sexual relationship with one of the neighbor girls. Don was about sixteen. He was being admonished about this affair and all the mishaps that might occur. After listening to his step father, Don blurted out, "My god, Pa, what would you do if a girl takes down her pants and throws her body in your face?" Vic stammered in his deep voice, "Well...well...I guess I would have taken advantage of the situation," whereupon his wife landed on both of them with a barrage of words that left both of them red-faced. "Vic, how could you possibly agree with Donald, you are supposed to set a positive example, etc." For me as a teenager, coming from a very conservative and religious family, I could not imagine such a conversation taking place at our dinner table.

There was a man who came to fish each summer from Montana. He originally piled the cork line, but later piled the lead line after the skipper assigned me to the cork line. Montana was what you would expect a cowboy to be. He spoke very slowly in a deliberate cadence. His face, set with dark brown eyes, looked as though he had spent most of his life outdoors, just like Vic, and I liked him right away. Montana knew all the various jobs on the boat and he explained everything to us greenhorns in his deliberate way. He never talked down to us, treating everyone equally. He took a great deal of time showing Don and me how to repair holes in the net with a large wooden needle laced with twine. Every once in a while, when I started making a bag out of a hole repair and could not get it to close up, Montana patiently undid all of my work and got me going in the right direction again. A bag was a bowl shaped bulge that would form in the net if not sewn properly. Beneath his calm demeanor I sensed a powerful man that I would want on my side in a fight.

After a hard day of fishing and with all the dinner dishes cleaned and put away, Montana taught me to play cribbage. The boat was usually anchored in a sheltered harbor for the night. Sometimes Vic's brother would tie up alongside. The galley was quite small, the boat had a beam of thirteen feet with a foot and a half of walkway on each side. This left about ten feet for the galley, half for cooking and the rest was a booth-like area where everyone had to slide in for a place to sit. After dinner, some of the guys would go to their bunks. This made seating more comfortable for card players. We spent many hours playing and the winner took on the next challenger. I never learned what sort of work Montana did when he was back in his home state. The next year when Montana did not show up the skipper told us he was badly burned in a work-related accident. He never came west to fish again.

The cook was a very likeable character. Always smiling and laughing, he had voice that sounded exactly like the old film actor Andy Devine.

He even looked like him, with a rotund figure capped with a round jovial face and heavy jowls that flapped about when he moved quickly around the galley. His name was Ed Lavassar and he was a retired firefighter from the Seattle Fire Department. Always the first one up at 4 a.m., I would be right behind him. He made the coffee and toasted huge hand-cut slices of French bread in the galley oven, then slathered them with butter and piled them high with strawberry jam. This is something I enjoy to this day.

Being the first ones up, we chatted over our coffee and toast until the rest of the crew came crawling out of their bunks. The conversation usually circled around the previous day's fishing, how good it was or how bad, and how the new day was sure to bring lots of fish. He would mention what meals he was planning to prepare that day. I think he was testing me to see if I would like what he had on the menu, because he knew that I was the biggest eater on the boat.

Fishing started before dawn and after toast and coffee. Everyone, still not fully awake, went to his respective work area. The crew was fed in shifts as the workday began, so Don and I usually didn't get breakfast until after the closing of the first set sometime between 5 and 6 a.m. We would climb back over the stern into the main boat for our turn. We really looked forward to Ed's whopping breakfast of ham, bacon, eggs, sausages and pancakes, including more toast and coffee. We worked hard and we ate very well.

I loved the sea around the San Juan Islands and the bounty of silver, sockeye, Chinook, humpies and chums that it provided. Ed once asked me if I liked fish and said I sure did. He told me to set a silver or sockeye salmon aside and he would fix it for dinner. I tossed one out for him from the early morning catch and Ed cleaned it and hung it out in the rigging. He said it was best to air it out for the day to get rid of the fish smell. That night we had baked salmon that I will never forget. Ed baked it in a covered pan with all kinds of vegetables and spices I do not know. I think I ate half the salmon myself and from then on I would try to coax him into baking salmon almost every night until the other guys started to complain. The fish dinners also saved us a bit of money because the food costs were part of our total expenses before shares were divided at the season end. The fishing season lasted about four months.

I had known my boyhood friend Don since we both attended Highland Park Grade School. About 5'7" and of very slight build, his shoulders seemed to protrude from his chest giving his torso a concave appearance. His hair was black and combed straight back. He had an olive shaped head, which was also reflected in the curvature of his nose, and he had dark brown eyes set close together. While I was in the Army, Don worked in a foundry. This was extremely hard work and it hardened him physically. Don was a generous soul willing to share anything he had. Though Don was of small stature, he would not back down if confronted with a fight. A great outdoorsman, he was a natural hunter and fisherman. This ability enabled him to catch fish and game when everyone else was skunked.

On one of our fresh water game fish excursions we fished a small stream that flowed into the south end of Lake Kapowsin, near Eatonville, Washington. We fished it several times in the mid 1940s, when we were both about 16 years old. The stream was not very wide and could be crossed easily at any point in our knee-high rubber boots. Don quickly caught his limit of twenty trout and then he went to work on the whitefish. These fish had a very small, circular mouth, shaped like a suction cup. We used single egg hooks, which a single salmon egg concealed completely. You had to have a good feel of your fishing pole to tell when you had a nibble on your bait. A trout would hit hard and bend the tip of the pole. The Whitefish just sort of sucked the bait in gently. Don caught them every time and I was never able to land one.

Don's stepfather, Vic, had built a cabin on the shores of Lake Ohop just northwest of Eatonville in the early 40s. For many years Don and I fished opening day there, sometime in mid-April. At that time all the roads around the lake were rutted gravel and very dusty on dry days. One day we put our boat in at daybreak and after exhausting all of our efforts along the shoreline and landing only a few 14-inch trout, we decided to troll the middle of the lake using various spinners and spoons. Along the shore we had some luck with a small lure called a flatfish. Don put some tackle on his line known as tandem gear, which is a long series of shiny spoons with fake eggs and a hook at the end. We were freezing in the early morning chill so it was nice when sun finally came up and we motored out of the shadows of the eastern shoreline.

We made ourselves as comfortable as we could in the small motorboat and tried to catch a little shuteye while we trolled slowly to the north. We had fallen asleep in the morning sun, my pole off to one side and Don's pole straight up between his knees off the stern when—BAM! Don's pole gave such a jerk he almost lost it. There was all kinds of action in the water far behind the boat. Don gripped his fishing pole tightly as it bent and snapped up and down. He reeled in and we saw the big fish struggling hard to get off the line, leaping out of the water. Other boats closed in to observe the action and it took quite a while until Don got the fish close enough to the boat for me to net it. We had to be careful with the long stretch of tandem gear as it could easily come out of the fish's mouth. When I finally netted it and got it into the boat, Don held it up for all to see—a beautiful five pound. silver trout that many later said was the largest they had ever seen taken from that lake. Don took the fish home to show his parents and they enjoyed it for dinner.

There was a stream that flowed past the south end of Lake Ohop that connected with the outflow from the lake. Don and I fished that stream with some success as well. It was not very deep, so it was a big surprise when Don pulled a three-pound trout out of a 4-foot deep hole beneath a waterfall. He was actually standing at the top of falls, fishing the hole where the falls crashed into the pool. I was fishing the same hole at the base of the falls, and although I was getting some good bites, I couldn't hook anything. The rain began, eventually coming down in sheets when Don hooked the big one. He was trying to make his way down to where I was so he could land it when he slipped on a wet rock and suddenly disappeared. He was swept over the falls. The next thing I saw was a head popping up out of the water near my line. Don still had the pole in his hand and the fish was still on his line. He staggered to the shore and finally landed it. We both marched home dripping wet, but triumphant with fish in hand.

The falls Don went over with a fish on the line

On one of our trips to Lake Ohop on a dusty gravel road, we looked out the driver's side window to see a wheel and tire passing us by. We realized the left rear wheel had come off and it was passing us as if we were in a race. Miraculously, we didn't tip over, and continued to run steady on three wheels until we caught up to the wheel and stopped. We discovered that the cotter pin that held the nut in place had broken, and somewhere back down the road was the nut that held the tire in place. After searching extensively we could not find it. We were miles from any gas station, and farms in the area were spread far apart. Don said that farmers usually have a lot of equipment and parts lying around. He decided to go from farm to farm to try and find a nut that would fit. I was to stay with the car while he trudged off. About an hour and a half had gone by and he returned with a handful of nuts in various sizes. One by one we tried them and by some miracle, one of the nuts fit perfectly. Feeling really good about being able to collect what was needed, we secured the nut with a new cotter pin and continued our journey.

Back on the *Loyal* there always seemed to be one shirker on every boat crew. We had one and his name was Hans. For some reason, Hans could not keep up with the rest of the seine pilers working alongside him. Because all of our livelihoods depended on the net, the rest of us would really come down on Hans, but no matter how much we chided and cajoled him, he simply could not keep up. It got to the point where I thought someone was going to toss him overboard. They bumped him and thumped him and cursed him to no avail. At supper both the skipper and the crew admonished him. He lasted only one season.

The summer morning beauty of the San Juan Islands is nearly beyond description. Don and I were always out in the skiff just as the dawn was breaking, when there was not a breath of wind. The vast body of water was like a mirror reflecting everything that was happening in the sky. The firmament was filled with scattered clouds, spaced evenly and shaped like popcorn balls. When the sun came up over the Cascade Mountains in the distance, it bathed the bottoms of these puffy clouds in deep reds that contrasted against the deep bluish indigo of space around them. Minute by minute the colors kept changing, from red to dark orange, then light orange to yellows. The sky began to resemble a giant piece of fabric imbedded with colored lights. This glorious show would slowly and regretfully end as the sun rose above the cloud layer.

Don and I sat in the stillness of the morning, waiting and watching from the skiff for signs of salmon going by. The skipper had instructed us that if the fish were schooled up they usually made a showing by finning near the surface. At the first sign of fish, we shouted to the main boat, which caused great excitement as the news reached the crew. To close the seine, Don or I tossed our line to a man on the boat and then the pursing of the net began.

The First Job

One morning, as light began to fill the heavens and a breeze picked up creating a rippled texture on the water's surface, Don and I got as comfortable as we could, taking turns to catch a snooze while the other watched for finners. The stillness was broken only by the chugging of the big boat's engines. Suddenly, the peace of the morning was shattered by a loud whooshing sound as the water broke nearby revealing a giant fish, then another until we were surrounded by creatures that appeared to be as large as submarines. Some breached the surface and came down with a horrendous splash, just yards from the skiff.

Suddenly, out of the stillness, a great whooshing sound!

These giants of the sea, which can grow up to 33 feet in length and weigh as much as 12,000 pounds, were known to fishermen then as blackfish and were sometimes shot at because they were after the same food we were—salmon. Blackfish chased the salmon and in the course of scattering them, it ended fishing for the day. When this happened, nets were pulled up and we went back to the big boat to mend them and play cards. It was a reprieve from the backbreaking labor of net hauling and fishing in general, but we thought about the salmon that we weren't catching, being caught instead by those enormous creatures.

It was years later that I learned that these blackfish are actually mammals, swimming in pods of 6 to 40, and today are known as orcas or killer whales. It was exciting and at the same time frightening to see these large animals so close to the skiff. Orcas are warm blooded, air-breathing mammals that can dive to depths of 100 feet. They could easily dive under the purse seine net. They have a shiny black skin over the upper portion of their bodies with the underside being pure white.

Behind the spout is a large vertical fin, giving the appearance of a shark. A pair of flippers and a powerful tail round out the projections. They propel themselves completely out of the water, turning over in mid air, to come crashing back down into the water on their backs. It was a chiaroscuro effect, in motion, with the flashing of black and white. Today, pods that enter the Sound and the waters of the San Juans are carefully monitored by marine biologists and various conservation groups out of concern for their safety.

Most of the seining was done off of San Juan Island near Cattle Point, also known as the Salmon Bank. The salmon tend to swim into the Straits of Juan de Fuca and head straight for the San Juan Islands. The banks north of Cattle Point are the ideal location for setting the seine.

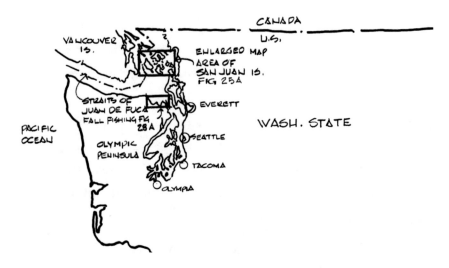

During the summer time, boats would be all lined up with their bows pointed toward open water, ready to toss the lead net at the first sign of fish. Each boat took its turn in the line—set the net, hold open for ½ hour to 1 hour—then the next boat would follow. Every once in a while someone jumped the line and there would be shouting and cursing between boats. On one occasion, where a line breaker cut off another boat, shotguns came out and the skipper in the boat that was cutoff was blasting away at the second boat's cork line as it was laid out within a few feet from the first boat's net.

Another incident of getting out of line resulted in two boats colliding. Fortunately the damage was slight, but in the collision, the men on the boats bounced around like billiard balls. A lot of cursing and shaking of fists ensued. The sight of a school of salmon excited some skippers to act without thinking.

The San Juan Islands

The San Juan Islands are a unique and beautiful group of islands, carved into various shapes by the glacier that covered the North American continent thousands of years ago. These islands are blessed with little rainfall and a great deal of sunshine. The glacier scraped many nooks, crannies and coves into the island coastline, some of it steep and rocky, exposed granite that plunges to 1000 feet beneath the water.

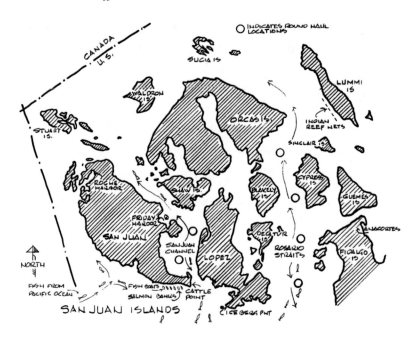

The San Juan Islands

The tides and currents can become ferocious and have been known to pull entire seine nets under if caught in the swift moving water. It happened to us once off Cattle Point when we held open a little too long. The lead net went down and Don and I struggled for two hours pulling it back into the skiff. As we rode the swirling current it pulled us miles from the main boat. Panic gripped us and my knees started to give way with the rush of adrenalin—the entire season of fishing was disappearing before our eyes.

Back on the *Loyal,* men struggled with the big net, which was also going down. If the net were pulled under far enough, it would be torn to pieces on the rocks and possibly snagged so it could not be retrieved. Don and I finally got the lead net up and we sped back to the big boat to help with the retrieval of the seine. All of us worked furiously with aching muscles and torn fingers until we finally got the net in. It had been torn badly and all the fish had escaped. We tied up to a large floating dock where the nets were off-loaded and everyone with needle in hand began the repair work.

When salmon came in to the San Juans and hit the salmon banks, they tended to split up and go off left and right. Some ran north in the San Juan Channel and others east, then north through the Rosario Straits, some heading for the big rivers of Canada. They passed by Lummi Island where the Indians fished with reef nets in the shallows. The Indians stood on small towers built in their boats, peering down into the clear waters. As fish swam over the net it was raised and the fish would be flipped into the boats.

In this area from the early 1900s up until 1935, fixed fish traps were constructed in the paths of migrating salmon. These traps worked 24 hours a day, trapping thousands of salmon and nearly destroying the runs. In 1935 laws were enacted eliminating the use of fixed gear that included the traps.

Not all of our purse seine sets were made with the setting of the lead net. There were times when large schools of salmon were spotted in one of the channels. On such occurrences, a round haul was performed. The skiff would take the end of the big seine and start the set. The big boat would quickly make a circle and come back to the skiff, pick up the end of the seine and immediately start to purse the net. Some of our best hauls were made in this manner in the waters of the Rosario Straits.

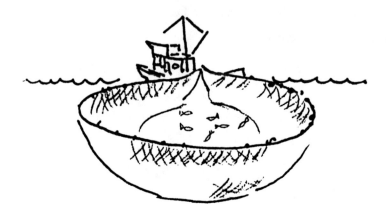

Pursing

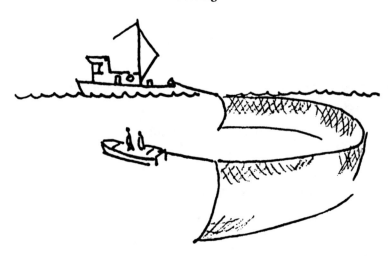

Round haul

Fishing did not end until sunset and even then we had to wait for a buyer to come by to unload our catch. This was done on the open water. The fish buyers tied up along side and a box was lowered into the hold of the *Loyal*. The boom of the buyer boat had a block and tackle attached to a winch. The box was loaded, raised and put on a scale to be weighed. When the fishing was good, this sometimes went on late into the night. We still had to eat our dinner, hop into the bunks and catch some shuteye so we could be up again at 4 a.m. the following morning. The buyers, to insure that fish were sold to them, often bribed the boat crews with a case or two of beer. Our skipper would take the beer, but would not allow any drinking until Friday when the boat was heading back to Anacortes for anchorage over the weekend.

Some weekends we would drive all the way back to Seattle to stay for two nights and then drive back to Anacortes on Sunday. This long drive was tiresome. Highway 99 had only two lanes and there were no freeways, so at other times we stayed on the boat for the weekend.

On one occasion, Don, Montana and I went into town to check out the excitement of a Friday night in Anacortes. We wandered about until we found a tavern that had live music and was packed with locals and fisherman from other boats. The patrons sat on long benches at picnic-like tables that were arranged around the dance floor. We purchased beer and sat down at a vacant spot that accommodated the three of us. There were people sitting on each side of us and across the table.

Don had been having a lot of words with Hans, the lazy one, during the week and he was still simmering with anger. Don struck up a conversation with another fisherman nicknamed Red who was sitting across the table. He was tall and sinewy with a narrow face, sharp nose and eyes set close together, his head topped off with reddish brown hair. Red was telling Don that he was so great with a knife that he could fillet a salmon right down to the bone with no loss of meat in a matter of seconds. Don, being in a bad mood, did not believe Red's phenomenal skills and after a few more beers the discussion became heavy and serious. Don kept telling Red he was full of bullshit and that nobody could do what he claimed. Montana and I tried to calm things down and told them to talk about something else. Red started to talk about cars and said he had enough money to buy a new car. He was going to Seattle the following weekend to buy a new Oldsmobile. Don countered that anyone working on a fish boat could not have made enough to buy a new car and that Red was still full of shit.

The breaking point was finally reached. Red got up, came around the table and Don had swung his feet out from under the table so they were face to face. Don was still seated and he was not very big, weighing about 140 pounds. Red grabbed him with both hands and picked him right up off the bench. Don was dangling in the air looking helpless, but what happened next surprised Montana and me. Don swung with a quick left and then a right, catching Red's right and left eyes. Red, still hanging on was sent reeling backwards onto the dance floor. The place looked like a bowling alley where someone had just made a strike. Bodies were everywhere. The music stopped, the bartender and bouncer were on the scene in seconds and we were all thrown out to a chorus of boos from the locals.

Don is yanked up out of his shoes!

Don had worn his slip-on shoes that evening and as we stood on the side walk, still dazed by the speed at which we were thrown out, Don said, "My shoes are still inside." We looked down to see bare feet on the pavement. I volunteered to try to find his shoes, but first I had to get by the bouncer and bartender. I pleaded with them both, said I was not looking for trouble, only Don's shoes. I had to crawl around under the table on the dance floor as the shoes had been scattered in the melee, all to the additional boos and taunts from the patrons. I found them both and we made our way back to the boat, thinking the entire distance how glad I was that Red didn't pull his knife to show us how quickly he could fillet Don.

The next weekend we all decided to go back to Seattle. I owned a 1948 Oldsmobile that I had arranged to be serviced at the dealership downtown. When I got there, I ran into Red, who was buying an Oldsmobile, just as he'd said. He was sporting two of the biggest black eyes I'd ever seen. Fortunately he didn't recognize me.

Fall Seining

In the months of October and November we took the seine boat to Discovery Bay to catch the big hook-nosed silvers that ran through there in the fall. Discovery Bay is located just west of Port Townsend. We fished behind Protection Island, between Beckett Point and Cape George.

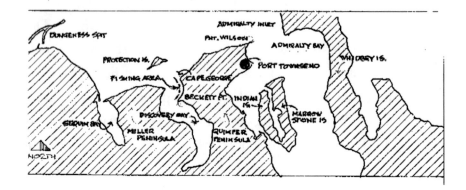

The fish we caught were big, but few and far between. The weather at times was very nasty and we were pelted with sleet and snow. Our fingers got so cold pulling in nets that we could barely feel them. Sometimes the net snapped hard against our fingers like a whip, causing them to ache with unbearable pain.

Once, our net drifted into a school of mud sharks. There were thousands of them, 18 to 24 inches long. They became entangled in the web of the net because of their small size and shape. We had to stop the net every few feet to pull them out and toss them overboard. It took several hours to bring the net in. This turned out to be the only winter seining season that I participated in and monetarily it was a flop. I looked at winter seining as a learning experience. We had a place to stay and we were well fed. In the warmth of the galley, the conversations and cribbage games gave us a feeling of camaraderie.

Rigged for Trawling

In the early spring the boat was rigged for trawling. This type of fishing brought in various species of bottom fish—sole, ling cod, true cod and red snapper. We fished the banks off the west coast of Vancouver

Island, from the mouth of the Straits of Juan de Fuca to as far north as the Queen Charlotte Islands.

Don and I had never done this kind of fishing, but our skipper gave us explicit instructions on what to do. I was to learn, later on, why there were not many men volunteering for this type of work. Working the winter season was like an insurance policy for getting a place on the boat for the next summer's seining season, and the skipper could then choose the men he knew were dependable, hard workers. The three brothers, Vic, John and Ben set off together, respectively, on the boats the *Loyal*, the *Betty June* and the *Yankee Maid*.

The weather can change very quickly during March and April as we were soon to experience. Our first stop was to load the hold with seven tons of crushed ice, because, unlike the boats of today, we had no refrigeration. Working a trawler was done with a crew of four. My favorite cook, Ed, did not come with us on this trip. The skipper had found another cook who we would soon have doubts about. I don't know if it was the rough seas or just his inability to cook, but we had many a lousy meal. The first thing the new cook prepared was a vegetable stew, in which the vegetables were overcooked and turned to mush. When he made fish dinners, the fish was not cooked all the way through. His sandwiches were OK, but it's hard to ruin a sandwich.

Our first encounter with bad weather occurred just as we entered the Straits of Juan de Fuca. Heading west around Dungeness Spit, the skipper had gone to his bunk, and Don and I were put in charge of the wheelhouse. The cook was in the galley preparing the evening meal. The strong, steady westerly wind was blowing into the Straits and the boat was taking solid green water over the bow. It shuddered and creaked as water crashed against the windows of the wheelhouse. The wind was blowing the tops off the waves as they peaked, making the sea all white.

Deep in the troughs, all you could see was green water.

As the *Loyal* rounded the Dungeness Spit a heavy swell hit us with tremendous force. The boat rolled and it looked like it was momentarily submerged. The skipper leaped out of his bunk and was at the wheel in seconds. He throttled the engine back and told us to hold it down and to throttle down more to keep the boat from diving into the waves. He briefly talked about pulling into Anacortes for an overnight stay, but quickly changed his mind, saying that it would probably still be blowing in the morning and he wanted to get to Neah Bay before night fall. While the noise of the crashing waves was frightening, the calm rasp of the skipper was reassuring and made us feel at ease.

After looking around, he told us to keep going and went back to sleep. Only a person who had spent most of his life at sea could sleep on the roller coaster we were riding. After a couple of hours, the cook came up and said supper was ready. We woke the skipper and he told Don and me to go ahead and eat first and when we finished we could relieve him.

The galley opened to the engine room, which you passed through to get to the bunks under the bow. To get to the galley you had to step out on deck and from the wheelhouse then back in through another door to the galley. In stormy weather, one had to time this move carefully. You wait until the boat is just coming off the top of a wave and then make a dash for it before the bow buries itself in the next wave. Hesitating could wash you overboard. The water temperature here, in wintertime, is about 45 degrees and a person without a thermal suit would last only a few minutes before hypothermia took hold. In a thrashing sea, there was no hope of swimming to the distant shore.

Stepping into the galley we found chaos. Things were flying all over the place. The fence around the stove didn't help and the cook and his apron were splattered. He staggered to get plates on the table, which also had a low rail around it. The cook had put together some kind of stew, served with bread and coffee, all of which went flying around the table if you didn't have them in hand. After a few bites I started to feel sick. The heat of the galley stove and the fumes coming up from the engine room were very oppressive. I had to get out. I jumped out onto the deck and ran behind the wheelhouse for protection from the wind and rain, the sea rushing down the decks on each side of the boat. Fortunately there was plenty of machinery and gear to hang onto and I fixed my eyes on the horizon until the nausea left me and I could go back to peck away at my supper.

Nightfall was upon us as we pulled into the harbor at Neah Bay. It was a strange but good feeling to motor into calm waters again. You would get so used to trying to keep your balance that the calm of the harbor seemed unreal, a stark contrast to the violence we had been subjected to for several hours. We dropped anchor and had a good night's sleep.

The next morning we were up early and the skipper explained the operation of a trawler. The net is shaped like a cornucopia—the throat, when open, being about 100 feet wide and the length about 150 feet. The open end of the net is connected to heavy steel cables on each side of the opening. These cables are connected to heavy-duty doors that are bolted together with metal plates. The doors are about four feet by six feet and four inches thick. They are set at an angle that will pull the net down to the bottom of the sea. They act like elevators on the wing of an airplane. The cable leading off from the door to the boat runs through a heavy metal single block that is attached to a davit on the deck. The cable then runs to a steel drum that is operated by a lever to let the net out or to bring it back in.

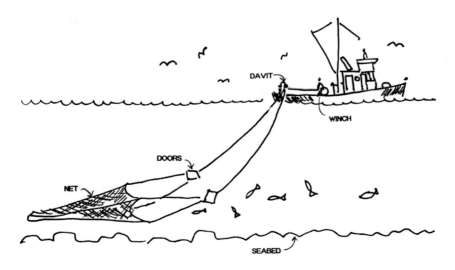

Trawling

The winch is driven by a power take-off from the main engine. Don and I were told to let the doors out at exactly the same rate of speed. If one door went out quicker than the other, there was the possibility of the other door dropping below the first and causing it to go into a circular motion, wrapping itself around the cable of the slower moving door. This twisting action can happen very quickly and shorten the cables to the point where they wrap around the propeller and shaft, leaving the boat helpless, far out at sea. All the instructions were firmly in mind. With the fear of losing the *Loyal* imbedded in our minds as well, we headed out of Neah Bay and into the Straits northbound up the Canadian coast for the fishing banks. The sea had calmed down, but the swells were still so deep we lost sight of the other boats as we slid to the bottom of each wave.

Don and I looked forward to the setting of the nets with great trepidation. This would be the first time for both of us to be operating the machinery of a trawler. We would be fishing in 60 to 70 fathoms of water and the net would be ½ mile to a mile behind the boat, depending on the depth of the sea.

The wind was now bringing patchy clouds from the west and blue sky was showing here and there. The sun came out and when the rays caressed the sea, it turned from a dull grey to a beautiful bluish green. The seagulls followed the boats with wailing cries, anticipating the feast they would soon enjoy. It took a few hours to get to the fishing grounds. When we arrived the skipper gave the signal to lower the nets. It was a long time before they reached the bottom. Don and I were careful to lower the net, and we took our time. The doors never crossed and we felt good about our achievement. The net was left out for a couple of hours or more before being hauled in. The same care had to be employed when bringing the net in and the skipper, with his vast experience, seemed to know when it was time to haul up.

While the net is on the bottom, the boat is somewhat stabilized in riding through heavy swell. The trawling speed is very slow—just the right speed to troll for salmon. The fishing boat was stocked with canned food to last 18 days. To amuse ourselves in the slack time and for variety in our diet, we rigged up a line and some gear and attached it to a bungee-like cord to try our luck at catching a fresh salmon for dinner. On more than one occasion we were successful and a delicious meal ensued.

Aboard the Loyal

The westerly swell was still running heavy from the storm that had just passed when the skipper gave us the signal to bring up the net. As this was the first time we had worked with the trawler gear, we did not know what to expect. It takes a long time to bring the heavy doors and net to the surface, and we could feel the pull of the net on the winches as they groaned and strained under the load. The boat would be lucky to make two sets in a day in the short hours of sunlight in March and April. If the weather were stormy, it made the days even shorter, the heavy cloud cover stealing the early morning and evening light.

The fish at 60 to 70 fathoms are under tremendous pressure so as they are brought up they bloat and become like floats. The closer to the surface, the lighter the pull became on the winches. Finally, there is no pull at all and with a great whoosh, the entire length of the net is floating on the surface, filled with bloated fish. The seagulls that had followed our boat were now diving by the hundreds into the net, plucking what they could through the mesh. To see a sight like this for the first time is unforgettable. It was a dramatic scene, with the bright blue-green of the water, seagulls with their white wings flashing, diving into the net trying to get a bit of the bounty we had brought up from the bottom of the sea. But now the real work was to begin.

The net, filled with fish, popped up like a cork.

The tail end of the net is brought close to the boat. It is pursed together with steel rings that hold the fish in the sock. We worked a cable around a length of the net, drew it up tightly and then with the boom and winch, raised that section of net onto the deck. The mechanism that held the pursed rings together was released and the fish cascaded over the entire deck of the boat. Soon we were knee deep in the slithering mass, and it was hard to keep our footing. The boat pitched heavily in the swells now that it wasn't moving and it made the work extremely difficult. Everything that you could imagine was brought up from the bottom. There were octopi, some stretching 13 feet across, halibut, wolf eels, ling cod, true cod, black cod, all varieties of sole, sea cucumbers, rocks and on some occasions segments of the backbone of a whale. The skipper took the whalebones to display at his home, but anything else that we could not sell was tossed back overboard.

Knee-deep in fish)

The skipper ordered one of us into the hold to start icing down the fish in bins below. The fish had to be sorted and packed between layers of ice, so I had to tunnel my way through the crushed ice to the forward bins. With the only light filtering down through the open hatch and through the mountain of ice, everything glowed a strange bluish-green. The tunnel through the ice to the bins was just large enough for a body to squeeze through and slide ahead into the workspace. Right behind me, the fish came tumbling down in great bunches. I had to work furiously to keep up, separating the various species then stacking and icing them.

Imagine yourself now, in a space not much larger than a coffin, sitting in a pile of fish. You can hardly see and the boat is being pitched and tossed about in the swells. Things get progressively worse when the fish are stacked in the bins. Under the weight of the ice the fish start to ooze fluids, which then drain into the bilge. The bilge water runs up under the big diesel engine and the heat from the motor warms the bilge water creating a stench that is unbelievable and beyond description. Being tossed around in this confined space while breathing these noxious vapors tend to make one ill, and so we limited our turns in the hold to half an hour.

After being in the hold that long, I would crawl out of the ice tunnel, my face green and lungs bursting, gasping for a breath of fresh sea air. It takes a few minutes to recover and then it's back to work with more and more fish piling up on the deck. Once the net was empty, it was reset and the work continued with one or the other of us icing the fish until the decks were swept clean.

The halibut we caught had to be thrown back as it is illegal to catch them in a net. Some weighed over 200 pounds and it took two of us to throw them back. We tossed the giant octopi and then watched them take off like underwater jets, trailing plumes of ink as camouflage.

However, the most dangerous creature to get off the boat was the wolf eel. Up to six feet long, with a mouth full of razor sharp teeth, their eyes looked just as mean as those teeth. If an eel came up near the bottom of the net, he was pretty much crushed by the weight of the fish on top, making him docile enough to handle, but if he was on top of the pile, watch out! The eels slithered all over the other fish like snakes. Don was trying to guide one over the side with a broom handle when the eel promptly bit the handle in half. Another one took a corner off the hold hatch. Seeing this fierce activity, we became very wary and protective of our limbs.

The ling cod, some weighing 50 to 60 pounds, had enormous mouths, opening wide as dinner plates. When trapped in the net, the lings must have thought they were in seventh heaven, surrounded by fish they could easily eat. I counted six true cod in the mouth of one ling, their tails sticking out as they thrashed about. The skipper wanted us to set the ling cod aside, clean them and cut their heads off before icing them down. In the cleaning process, we discovered their hearts continued to beat as the entrails lay on the deck. We disconnected the heart from the rest of the guts and set it on the deck to see how long it would keep beating. Some lasted for over an hour.

The last chore was to clean up the decks with large scoop shovels. It was sad to see the destruction of so many small fish. They were not marketable, so they were simply scooped up and tossed overboard. The seagulls went wild, screeching and diving for the tiny morsels. We then pumped the bilge in hopes of getting rid of the horrible odor but to no avail—it never seemed to leave the boat completely.

We fished each day and tried to get all of our gear up from the deep in time to get into a harbor on Vancouver Island. The favored harbor is a place called Esperanza Inlet. We had to get in before nightfall because there were no lights to guide us past all the huge rocks. Once safely in the harbor, we dropped anchor for a night of rest. The crew's quarters were under the bow and there were bunks for eight, which were all filled when we were seining. The skipper had a bunk in the wheelhouse. There was no shower on the boat and in the very tiny head there was a toilet and sink with just enough room to turn and sit down. After 18 days on the trawler, we were as ripe as the fish.

The bunks were stacked so there was just enough room to slip in, if you awoke suddenly at night and raised your head, you would bump into the bottom of the bunk above you. The work was hard and tiring and with the fresh sea air you usually fell asleep as soon as you hit your bunk.

There were days when we didn't get all of our gear up before nightfall and this meant we had to anchor and spend the night out in the ocean. In about 30 fathoms of water, we would release the steel cable that passed through a steel chock from a drum that was driven by the power take-off from the main engine. All of this was on the bow of the boat just above where we slept. But the sea never sleeps, and consequently, neither did we.

The huge swells in the open ocean came in steadily from the west. The boat rode like a roller coaster, slipping off the top of a wave like a fast elevator would send your stomach upward. The speed of the descent was amazing, until you were at the bottom, then just as quickly going back up with your stomach pressed down. The most frightening experience was at the top of the swell, when the boat met the end of the anchor chain. The line tightened abruptly and there would be a giant KABOOM! as the boat tried to lift the anchor. With all of this happening just over our heads, going on all night long, there was no way anyone could sleep waiting for the next KABOOM! You had to hang on to the sides of the bunk to keep from being thrown out. I thought for sure the bow would break off or the anchor line would part, but somehow we made it through those sleepless nights.

When we anchored in the ocean, we didn't have to run far to the fishing grounds so it assured us that we would finish early the next day and get safely into harbor the following night for a good night's sleep. It is amazing how much of a beating the body can take when young and still put in another full day of work. So now, many years later after a few hours of yard work, I am continually surprised when I wake up with badly aching muscles and bones.

On one occasion when we made it back into the inlet safely, we went to bed early. When we awoke the next morning, the skies were bright and sunny, but all the boats were covered with several inches of snow and all the trees around the harbor were wearing cloaks of white, their dark green limbs poking out in contrast. The water here in Esperanza Inlet is a beautiful deep green and all around the shore, trees grow right to the water's edge. For entertainment, we engaged in a snowball fight amongst the boats. After breakfast we pulled anchor and motored back out to the fishing grounds. We all hoped that the snowstorm would not be followed by another while we were trawling. It would have made the work miserable. The skies remained blue that day, but with the clearing came colder temperatures and a sharp wind that heightened the waves dramatically. Fortunately for us the weather held and another good day of fishing was had.

Distress Call

One day we received a distress call from John on the *Betty June*. Their experienced men had crossed their net's elevator doors and the cables were wound around the propeller and shaft. One of the men let his side of the net out faster causing the doors to spiral, twisting the cables and then wrapping around the propeller. Fortunately the net was not far behind the boat. It took us sometime to locate the *Betty June*, and it was dusk by the time we joined them, and we worked to get a line between the boats in the heavy, rolling seas. Before depth finders, a light line with a lead ball was used for sounding out the depth of uncharted waters. The idea was to toss the line completely over the distressed vessel so the men on the *Betty June* could retrieve it. To the end of the sounding line, we attached a heavy towline that we could then attach to the stanchion, which is amidships on the boat *Loyal.*

I stood on the deck, trying to keep my footing, whirling the lead ball for a toss across the *Betty June*. The sea was not cooperating and we had to keep the boats a fair distance apart to avoid crashing together. The lead ball made a whirring sound that rose above the wind as I twirled it. My first shot missed and I quickly gathered up the line for a second try.

After several hard twirls, I let go just at the right moment. The line flew far over the top of the *Betty June*, settled down across the deck and was quickly gathered in by the crew. The men secured the towline and we were off to Neah Bay, but between the high swells and the fact that the *Betty June* was dragging her net, it was late night by the time we arrived. We maneuvered her as close to shore as we could, and the plan was to beach the boat so the crew could work on freeing the cables from the prop. The tide was in so were able to get the *Betty June* close to shore.

When the tide went out, two of the men on the *Betty June* started working on the cables as soon as the prop was exposed. They were in water up to their waists when they started to unwind the cables and worked through the outgoing tide, finishing just as the tide came back in. You could hear all kinds of curse words echoing around the bay as the men worked. The *Betty June* was a much older boat than the *Loyal* and was equipped with a giant two-cylinder engine that, when running, made a sound like "ka-punk, ka-punk, ka-punk," the frequency of the sound rising and falling, echoed around the enclosure of the bay. To step into the engine room of the *Betty June* was like a trip to a museum. The engine was festooned with dials and valves made of shiny brass, the two enormous cylinders of the engine working up and down noisily.

The skipper, John, liked his drink and I believe the crew was selected for the same reason. I suspected that drinking also had something to do with the crossing of the doors. John didn't look like his brother Vic in any way. He was a much smaller, thinner man with a narrow face that was reddened by drinking and exposure to the severe environment. He took everything in stride, however, and was very calm through this disturbing experience.

One of John's crew, a man named Smitty, had a stocky build and wore a flat cap with a button-down bill. His hair was gray and it tufted out all around under his cap. It appeared that he never shaved and his graying, ungroomed beard grew in all directions as well. He also had a harelip and a number of his front teeth were missing. Together, these features gave him a very grisly appearance, and between the harelip and the missing teeth, his speech had a twang that made him difficult to understand. He loved to curse and everything he encountered was named with one of his favorite words. By comparison, Smitty's assistant looked so normal standing next to him, that there was nothing about him that I can remember. I never did see the cook.

Rogue Wave

Once, the *Betty June* was hit by a rogue wave while hauling in the net. The weight of the net held the boat down when the wave came over the stern. The men had to hang onto the winch equipment to keep from being washed overboard, struggling in the waist deep water. The greatest fear for most fishermen is falling into the water.

The waterproof gear we wore was designed to keep us dry. The boots come up to your knees, a slicker bib overall goes down over the boots to the ankles and the top part of the overalls to the chest. There is a slicker overcoat on top of all this that comes to below your waist and if you fell overboard, there was no way to pull off your boots under the bulky gear and they would fill with water and pull the victim under before a line or safety ring could be tossed.

Vic told us of a time they were trawling off the coast when they pulled up a Navy plane that was lost at sea during WWII. They radioed the Coast Guard with the plane's number, and the Coast Guard called the Navy. The Navy told the finders to let it drop back to the bottom. Their official papers had listed the plane as lost at sea and they didn't want to open a file that had been long closed.

As our 18-day trip came to a close, we headed through the Straits of Juan de Fuca to meet the fish buyers in Anacortes. Once there, the fish boxes were lowered into the hold, and once again, Don and I pitched the fish into the boxes, sorting out the species. Each species brought a different price. The petrale and other sole varieties supported the best price, then the red snapper, rockfish and cod. The fish at the bottom of the bins were unrecognizable, having been caught during the first few days out. They were crushed under the pile of ice and other fish making them grotesque and very flat.

The smell was nearly unbearable. The fish were cleaned and sold by the buyer as fresh fish, just in from the sea, but in fact some of these "fresh fish" had been under ice for 17 days. For this trip, we each made $25 as our share of the profits, but at least we had food, lodging and an unforgettable experience to take home. We made one more excursion to the fishing grounds that season and broke even, managing to pay for fuel, ice and food. Some fishing days are better than others!

A New Job

After the fishing season was over, Don and I worked on his Model A to get it up and running. We were in the street in front of the garage with our heads under the hood trying to adjust the timing of the engine. A friend of Don's parents came by for a visit. He spotted us and asked, "You guys want a job?" We looked up to see a man over six feet tall with glasses, wearing a strange looking hat. The crown of the hat was woven as if made of a straw-like material and the brim was loose and floppy and hung partially over his glasses. "What kind of job?" we asked. Looking us straight in the eye he said, "Steeplejacking."

Don informed me that the family friend's name was Harold. We said we didn't know anything about that kind of work, and Harold said, "You don't have to know anything. I'll teach you." I was to learn later that our inexperience and naiveté would serve us well. He told us he would pay two bucks an hour, and after my meager pay in the Army and what little Don and I made from fishing, it sounded like we were on our way to our first fortune. Don said he could only work for about a month because he had received his draft notice and was scheduled to report to the Army. This arrangement appeared to be acceptable to the man in the hat.

We soon learned that Harold's company was called H.A. Sommers Steeplejack. Harold was an exuberant, outgoing guy, always upbeat. He talked a mile-a-minute and wanted to know if we were both strong, because the first job was running a scaler. The job, located at West Coast Wood Preserve on Harbor Island in Seattle, was to scale off rust from the exterior of creosote storage tanks and once clean, to paint them. Neither one of us knew what a scaler was, but Harold assured us that anyone could run one—you just need to "have a lot of strength." Having just finished very strenuous work on the fishing boat, we both knew we could handle any job requiring muscle.

As soon as I was introduced to the scaler I was ready to quit. The machine was operated electrically and must have weighed thirty to forty pounds. It had a number of rotating chains on a drum and it whirled about at a high rate of speed. We were instructed to hold the machine up against the metal tank with the drum rotating and the whirling chains would knock off the rust. By the middle of the day our arms felt ready to fall off along with the rust and we anxiously looked forward to a break and luckily, Harold soon came by and said, "Let's go to lunch!" His bouncy, animated conversation and some lunch revived us and we went at it again until quitting time and by then my arms were numb.

But as the days went by our muscles grew stronger and the tanks got cleaned. Harold came and told us, "Now we're going to paint them." We asked him where the ladders were to reach the top of the tanks and he said, "We don't use ladders, we use bosun's chairs, some lines, pulleys and blocks." This was our first exposure to the tools of a steeplejack. Harold brought out all the gear and we had a lesson about lines, the chairs and how to use a mouse. The mouse is a loop of rope that you throw into the line over the hook that holds the chair. The line binds on itself and keeps you from free falling to earth. I immediately thought of many long past dreams about free falling from cliffs and other high places. This was a dream that had recurred to me many times and I thought, "My god, is it really going to happen?"

"How do you get to the top of the tank?" we asked. Harold explained,

"You take this line with a hook on it and toss it up over the edge of the tank and then pull the block and tackle up. There's another hook attached to the top block and you drop this over the edge of the tank as well. Get into the chair with a paint bucket and a brush and pull yourself up to the top where you will start, painting your way down the tank, carefully releasing and redoing the mouse at each drop."

I was paralyzed with fright at the prospect of working this high up in the air—these tanks were probably twenty to twenty-four feet high. I took a deep breath and pulled myself up, determined not to look down. Trussed up in this sitting position on the chair, I painted furiously to get back to the ground, and when I finally did and tried to stand up, fear had cramped my stomach muscles so tightly I couldn't straighten up. I shuffled around doing the duck walk until my muscles relaxed and I could stand up again. When I recovered, I slid the hook on the top of the tank over with a jerk and proceeded with my next drop. After a week of this I became accustomed to it and was working like a pro. I learned to diligently inspect all of the lines and gear that my life hung on and no two jobs were alike, which kept the work interesting.

The mill operator decided that he wanted all of the overhead ducts inside the building painted and Harold appointed me for the job. They were about 30 feet in the air and I asked him how I was supposed to get up there. Harold pointed to an overhead, grated walkway that was barely visible in the dimly lit building. I peered in the darkness and wondered how in the world I could see what I was to paint. We found a spot where I could transfer myself to the duct.

When I asked Harold how I was supposed to stay on the rounded ducting, He said, "Just ride it like a horse and keep shuffling yourself backward along the duct." I thought Harold was crazy. What if I came to a spot that was rusting internally that could not be seen? He assured me that it was strong enough to hold my weight, pointing out all the vertical supports that hung from the ceiling.

I made my way up, hopped onto the duct, and started painting. It was difficult to reach around to paint the underside, and getting around the vertical supports was a challenge to figure out. I learned to balance with my bucket of paint and brush in hand and soon had a system down, making good progress. I still was fearful of finding a weak spot in the duct and have the whole thing come crashing down, but as I moved along nothing untoward happened, my confidence grew and I rode the three hundred foot length, finishing the job.

The mill owner told Harold that the large gantry cranes had cracks in the metal plate supporting the turntable and wanted them welded along with all the rivets, which had become loose in their holes. The work had to be done at night so I volunteered to assist the certified welder. I was always interested in welding and thought I might learn something about it. The bright blue arc of the welder's torch had fascinated me since I had seen one as a child.

My job was to move his equipment around and to keep a fire extinguisher handy to protect against any fire that might be started by the shower of sparks. There were large amounts of lubricating grease around the main gear on the turntable, presenting a potential fire danger. This job went on for several nights and the work, for me, was boring. To stir up a little excitement, the welder let me try bit of welding. He instructed me to keep the gap of the arc constant so the rod wouldn't weld itself to the metal, and I found that mastering this was an art. In my inexperience, after getting stuck a few times, I turned the tools back over to the real welder. Though I was disappointed that I didn't pick up the knack of it quickly, I was to learn later that to weld properly requires a great deal of practice and good welders are worth their weight in gold.

The Water Tower

Don and I were sent to a job in downtown Seattle. In the early 1950s there were several old buildings that had large water tanks on the rooftops. These water tanks fed a fire suppression system within the structure. Harold won the bid to replace the roof of one of these tanks.

On top of an eight-story building, we proceeded to dismantle what was left of the old tank roof. Many tanks were made of wood. The wooden roof had rotted and pigeons were nesting inside. There were pigeon droppings and nest remnants on the rafters, adding to the mess and complicating the job. We put on our gloves and worked carefully pulling the roof apart and lowering the pieces onto the building roof. The parts were too large to load into the elevator or to carry down through the stairway, so Harold came up with a plan. "We'll come back on Sunday when the building is empty and throw it all to the parking lot below." The building was located in Pioneer Square and in those days, on a Sunday it would be a rarity to see a car or anyone about. So early the next Sunday we began tossing the sections of roof structure over the side.

We were glad to see them break into small pieces because then it was easy to load into a truck. Today this area has been revitalized and many of the buildings have neat shops, restaurants and art galleries, which attract many tourists. I wonder what Seattle's Department of Land Use and Construction would say if someone would attempt to clean a building in the way we did it.

The new roof was prefabricated in small sections in Harold's shop. The parts could be easily transported up in the freight elevator. The design was conical with a king post in the middle. It went together very quickly and before long, we were nailing on the asphalt shingles. This proved to be an exhilarating operation. We were eight stories above the ground, plus the height of the water tower, nailing shingles on the tank roof, with the tank sitting on the very edge of the building itself. We tied a rope around our waists and then onto the king post and worked our way around the circular cap. We both breathed a sigh of relief when this job was finished.

Time passed quickly, and Don got his call from the draft and left for the Army. I missed him because we worked so well together. We enjoyed exchanging stories, jokes and the laughter.

The Old Saw Mill

After Don left for the Army, I kept working for Harold doing whatever work was available. Harold had hired a man named Jack, who was about 37 and who could not construct a single sentence without an expletive. Everything was "f" this or "f" that and so on. He smoked continuously, coughing and gasping for air, swearing each time he had to catch his breath. Jack stood about 5'10" and had a dark complexion with dark brown eyes. He looked as though he shaved only once a week and his black, stubbly beard made him look particularly fierce. He was an expert with block and tackle, lines and rope and he knew how to rig up high. Our first job together was to paint all of the smoke stacks and the sawdust burner at a sawmill in Eatonville. It was summertime and the Northwest was experiencing a rare, rainless summer.

Jack and I rode the conveyor belt, standing on the lumber scraps right up to the top of the burner, carrying all of our drop gear, buckets, paint and brushes and just before the scrap dropped into the fire below, we had to jump off onto a catwalk grating that wrapped around the top of the burner. We were young and indestructible, giving no thought to the danger and years later I wondered—what if one of us had gotten our feet tangled up in the scrap? It would have been instant cremation

Preparing to paint, we rigged our lines, got in the bosun's chairs, and started our drops. We had to keep a watch on wind directions while we painted, because a sudden change could mean our lines would be exposed to the hot ash and cinders that were flying out of the top of the burner. The lines could catch on fire, separate and we would be falling suddenly at a high rate of speed. The burner was about 50 to 60 feet tall and a fall from this height would be fatal. The wind did shift several times and we had to release the mouse quickly and descend, moving to the windward side of the burner.

The remnants of what I had painted as a young man are now rusting relics. While the mill was in operation, the sawdust burner was never shut down, burning all of the scrap wood left over from the cutting of logs into dimensioned lumber. The jumble of scrap would roll out of the mill on a conveyor belt, straight into the top of the cone-shaped sawdust burner, dropping into a hellish fire that burned twenty-four hours a day. Just before the lumber reached the conveyor belt there was a platform where two men stood plucking stove-sized chunks and tumbling them into a truck below to take into town to sell as firewood. Seeing this wood made me think of my parents' home, because we used the same cuts of wood in a coal/wood burning gravity furnace located in the basement that heated our living space.

The burner was made of sheet metal and got extremely hot. By the time we made one drop it felt as if our toes were on fire, right through the heavy boots. We painted next to each other, and together each drop covered a swath twelve feet wide. The paint used could withstand several hundred degrees Fahrenheit before igniting, but as we applied the paint to the metal, it smoked, spewing fourth greenish gray fumes that, I am sure, were toxic. We had no masks, and we hacked and sputtered all the way down. I painted faster than Jack, because I hated the burning sensation on my toes, which were always in contact with the side of the burner because of the burner's tapered shape. I just wanted to get off the damn thing. Painting ahead of Jack created a problem when the fumes from my swath wafted up into his face. He cursed and yelled at me to slow down and I yelled back at him to speed up.

We discovered we had another problem. When the brushes hit the hot metal, some of the paint exploded and spattered into our face, which burned terribly. I had visions of having a pock marked face for the rest of my life. At a small drugstore in Eatonville, we explained our problem to the pharmacist who sold us a can of pure lanolin, which we applied to our faces up to 1/8" thick. This worked fine, but at the end of the day our faces were covered with grease and pockmarked with black spots. What a frightening pair! We were staying at Vic Carlsen's cabin on Lake Ohop, which was close to Eatonville. It had cold water only, so we had to start a fire to heat water before we could wash our greasy spotted faces. We wanted to look reasonably clean before we went out for our evening meal at the local restaurant.

After finishing the painting of the sawdust burner, we had to paint the smoke stacks on the main mill building. I believe there were five stacks in all and they protruded some thirty feet above the sloping metal roofline. When we finished painting the stacks, we had to go inside the building and continue painting them all the way down to the boiler breechings.

One of the stacks had a steam whistle which blew at the start of the day, at noon and in the evening at quitting time. Jack told me to start painting the one with the whistle, and for some reason, it terrified me to think of sitting in the bosun's chair next to this whistle. As a child, I was terrified of loud noises. We lived near Greenlake in Seattle and during the Fourth of July fireworks displays everyone seemed to have a pocketful of firecrackers. They would light and toss them about indiscriminately, and on one occasion, a firecracker was tossed in my direction and I ran into the path of an oncoming car. It was a miracle that I wasn't killed. No one understood how much I hated those loud noises.

We arrived long before the Mill started up to take advantage of the cool morning. We rigged our lines on the stacks, pulled ourselves up with the paint and brushes and began our drops. I worked furiously because I didn't want to be at the top of my drop next to that blasted steam whistle. I didn't know what time it was, but I knew it was due to go off at any minute and the anticipation was agonizing. The mill workers were arriving and the whistle was puffing and dripping, almost alive, like a dragon waiting to strike. Of course, whenever it finally did blow, it scared the hell out of me. I finished the stack before noon and moved onto the stack furthest from that screaming steam whistle.

We finished all of the exterior stacks and moved inside the building, and with the summer sun on the metal roof outside and the heat of the boiler inside, this was as close to burning in hell as I ever wanted to be. We rigged planks among the roof trusses to paint the upper part of the stacks, tying our chairs off to various structural members to make our drops to paint down to the boiler breechings. It got so hot near the breechings our brushes caught fire. After that experience we carried a bucket of water to dip our brushes into as they were set aflame a number of times. No longer the naïve person I was when I took on this work, I resolved that if this type of job ever came up again, I would refuse it. Sweat poured off our bodies, soaking our clothes and melting the lanolin on our faces, scaring a few of the mill workers with our bizarre appearance. After finishing this hellish job we celebrated, happy to have survived.

I have gone by the mill in recent years and it still stands as a ghost of its former days of glory. It was sad to see the place where many men were employed during the heyday of the timber industry. The timber in the area was all logged off, the mill closed. Today, when logging companies contract to log forests in the state, they are required to replant those areas and tourists who pass through can see posted signs indicating the year of harvest and replanting.

More Stacks

Harold was low bidder and won a contract to paint the stacks at the U.S. Plywood Mill located on the southeast end of the Ballard Bridge. The company wanted us to inspect the stacks prior to painting. A machine was rented that was gas-driven and had a drum wrapped with several hundred feet of steel cable. I was to hoist Jack up the outside and then he would rig up inside the stack and I would slowly lower him so that he could inspect the inside of the stack from top to bottom, stopping periodically. Everything went fine on the way up, but on the way back down, we had a near disaster.

About a third of the way down, Jack yelled at me to stop and the machine refused to brake. The cable just kept slipping, letting out line. I threw the motor into reverse and instead of stopping, all it did was slow his descent. Through a metal clean-out door at the bottom of the stack, I could hear Jack cursing as he banged from side to side, which loosened years of accumulated soot and carbon. The resulting noise combined with Jack's swearing from inside the stack was horrendous, and funny in a macabre sort of way.

I kept pressing the engine in reverse, and finally what appeared through the clean-out door was an apparition. Poor Jack was thoroughly black with soot—his eyes, ears, nose and mouth, hands and all of his clothing were black. His eyes looked like two red dots peering out of the black mask of his face. He could easily have joined a minstrel show. His teeth where still white in contrast as he spewed his voluminous vulgar vocabulary at me. I simply told him that the blasted machine was not working properly and we took it back to the rental store. After a great deal more cursing and arguing, we were given a newer, larger machine to finish the necessary work.

Damn The Torpedoes

At the Bangor Naval Station near Bremerton, we were to paint all of the structural steel trusses that supported the roof of a storage building for Navy torpedoes. The building was partly underground and a ramp led downward to the storage area. The concrete walls were earth-bermed up to the roofline. I estimated that the distance from the storage room floor to the bottom chords of the trusses was twenty-five to thirty feet. The building was sited so that if the torpedoes exploded, the force of the blast would be directed upward and any horizontal force would be contained by the concrete walls and earth berms. The place was poorly lit and the floor was always flooded with water. This was to insure that no sparks would accidentally set off the torpedoes. The Navy man told us that all the tools they used in the area were made of brass to avoid sparking. He carefully instructed us not to drop any of our metal tools or buckets while working above the torpedoes arrayed menacingly in their storage spaces in a vertical position, the nose cones pointing directly at us. We crawled through the structural maze of trusses above, painting as we went. But because we had to be so careful, the work went so slowly that our boss cursed us for taking too much time. He finally hired two more hands to help. One was an African-American who kept us amused with all of the various things he pictured that could happen if we accidentally dropped a bucket of paint on one of the ominous torpedoes. This was another job I was happy to leave, body intact.

One of my hardest jobs was straightening a stack that was bent in the middle of its towering height. It was located at a sawmill in Sumner, Washington. It protruded from the top of a sloping sheet metal roof. The building that supported it was about 30 to 40 feet high, with the stack rising an additional 50 or 60 feet above the roof. Evidently, rust had weakened the stack in the middle and it had tilted slightly after strong southerly winds had battered it.

We took careful measurements of the roof slope so a flat platform could be constructed where steel scaffolding would rise to surround the smoke stack. Erection of the scaffolding was done by hand, raising one piece at a time by line and a single block pulley, since cherry pickers had not made their appearance. There was no leverage advantage with this single line. My boss Harold was on top, bolting the scaffolding together and we kept at it for fourteen hours, finishing it in one day. Sections of new stack were manufactured by Stack Steel to fit around the existing stack. These were made in a half-round shape and were about five feet tall. Harold, prior to ordering the steel, sent me up the scaffolding to test the stack. He wanted to know where the steel was sound, and where rust had started and ended so he could have an accurate measure as to how much steel plate was needed. I was given an electric drill with what seemed like a mile of extension cord to punch holes in the stack to test for rust and weak points. I slowly worked my way up the scaffolding, drilling and taking notes.

From the top, the view of Mt. Rainier and the valley below was spectacular. There were no safety nets or straps to save me in case I fell, and the height was dizzying, so I was careful not to look down, instead concentrating on what had to be done. Years later, working as an architect, this experience of concentration was instrumental in enabling me to focus on a complicated project and see it through to fruition. I pulled a plank up with me to stand on at each level, then I would set up, drill my holes and make notes. The needed replacement steel was calculated and ordered.

When the pieces arrived, I was worried that they would have to be pulled up by hand. Harold, however, had rented a rig similar to the one I had trouble with at U.S. Plywood, and I looked at it with apprehension. Fortunately, it worked just fine. The trick turned out to be maneuvering the steel jackets up and inside of the scaffolding to be welded in position around the old stack. The jackets were half rounds so only one half of the stack was welded at a time. This work went quite slowly, but eventually we made it up to the bent sections. In order to straighten the stack we had to adjust the tension of the existing guy wires near the top of the stack. The wires were anchored to cement blocks far out in the yard. We chose a windless day and we began by loosening the wires on one side while tightening them on the other, and fairly soon we had straightened the stack. The jacketing and welding resumed until we were well past the area of the damage and into good metal again. With the stack repaired, the scaffolding procedure was reversed and the job completed.

There was a tremendous sense of accomplishment in straightening this smoke stack. When we first arrived at the site, I thought, "How in the world are we going to straighten this thing out?" It was a great learning experience for me, one that I still look back on when confronted with difficult situations.

Harold gave the owners a bill for four thousand dollars, and the owners were appalled. This was 1953 dollars, and at an inflation rate of 4% annually, this would be about thirty thousand today—still a good price for the unusual and dangerous work. In fact, if OSHA and WISHA, the national worker-safety organizations, had been in existence then, they would never have allowed the work to proceed as we had done it. The cost today might be closer to fifty thousand dollars.

Working for Harold

Harold made a great deal of money contracting these very odd, difficult jobs. He always kept a pocketful of cash and was generous in taking us out to lunch or dinner. There was a place in White Center where he spent much of his time. In those days, "blue laws" were in effect throughout the State of Washington, prohibiting the sale of liquor unless food was also served. To circumvent the law, there sprang up a number of watering holes called bottle clubs. You could bring your own hard liquor. They put your name on the bottle and then you would order various mixers that cost about a dollar. When you were done with your visit, the bottle would be marked with your name and how much was left. The White Center club that Harold belonged to was Desimone's Athletic Club, located in a Quonset hut on 17th Avenue.

Harold made arrangements for me to join the club, and I learned that it was more than just a drinking club. There was a card room in the back as well as some one-armed bandits in the hut. The stakes in the card games were extremely high. Harold related how he lost fifteen hundred dollars in one evening. This was a large amount of money in the 1950s.

I remember going to another bottle club that was located on a boat in the Salmon Bay area of the Hiram Chittenden Locks. It was called *Hernando's Hideaway* after a song that was popular at the time. They had even incorporated a password knock (three times) and a slot in the door opened at eye level where you would be asked several questions. When it was determined that you were not a cop or an undercover agent, you were let in. There was music, dancing and of course, drinking. Desimone's in White Center was raided a few times, and eventually all bottle clubs disappeared as quickly as they had come into being.

Working with Harold was a valuable education. I learned a lot about the practical aspects of construction, and because of the difficult, strenuous nature of the work, I learned the importance of going to college to learn something that would keep me closer to earth. Later, while practicing architecture, I had draftsmen working for me who would draw a detail that, after examining it I would ask, "Tell me, how do you think a carpenter is going to build what you have designed?" As the draftsman was halfway through his explanation he would realize it could not be done as drawn.

In 1954, I decided to register at the University of Washington to start school in the winter quarter. My decision to study architecture had never wavered from my high school days. Because I was a bit too late to start the fall quarter, I had to wait a couple of months with to nothing to do in the way of employment. This led me to the "Lazy B," aka Boeing Aircraft Co.

I went to the employment office and took an aptitude exam for work placement. I scored quite well. I told the interviewer my plans for going to school and that I only needed work for a couple of months. He was shocked, but must have been impressed that I was upfront with him. He hired me and I went to work as an expediter at Boeing's Renton plant..

Expediters had the freedom to wander through the entire plant, while other workers had to stay in their specific areas. It was my duty to find blue prints, templates and molds that would be needed somewhere in the plant. Workers would come to my desk and make a request and if we did not have it on file, I was sent out to find it.

At the Renton Plant, I carpooled with three Boeing supervisors, which was great because we could park inside in the restricted area. One of the supervisors was Sterling Sessions, who later became a Vice President of Boeing. The first 707 was being assembled under wraps at the Renton plant. The area was sealed off with large tarps that hung from the ceiling. The supervisors I rode with were heavily involved with this new jet aircraft. One day they invited me behind the curtain to view this creation of modern aircraft technology. As I looked over the aircraft, I was impressed by the large number of rivet placements over the entire body of the airplane. Each rivet had an inspector's stamp next to it and had been measured as to placement to within .0003 of an inch. I was thrilled to view all of this and be a part of the 707 airplane's development, even though my job was only locating the templates and drawings for the people who actually did the assembly.

One of the other supervisors was Stan, who lived next door to my parents. There was always a great deal of commotion emanating from Stan's house. I assumed that things were not always going well between him and his wife. She was a very stoutly built woman and I had visions of Stan being chased around the house with a frying pan. The other supervisors were aware of the situation and often kidded Stan about it.

One day, a little hamburger stand opened up around the corner from our house. All of us in the carpool worked swing shift so we would arrive home around midnight. The others, noting the new shop, said to Stan, "Stan, do something nice for your wife, buy her a hamburger." Stan replied, "Yeah, throw back the sheets and plant it on her back." This made it clear to me that all was not well at Stan's house—probably why he worked swing shift.

Soon winter quarter started at the University and I left Boeing. I thanked everyone for the opportunity to have worked with them. I packed up my things and started a five-year course in the study of architecture. Ever since I had taken Architectural Drawing at West Seattle High School, I wanted to be an architect. I had a wonderful teacher, Mr. Gorton, who would let me draw anything I wanted. This freedom of expression is exactly what a "wannabe" architect should have. Upon enrolling I was given an aptitude test. I never looked at the results of the test until after I graduated from the School of Architecture program. The results were as follows—Number 1 was Doctor, number 2 was Engineer, and number 3 was Architecture. This revelation confirmed that I was had been moving in the right direction.

U of W

In 1954 the School of Architecture was a five-year program to attain a Bachelor of Architecture degree. The program concentrated on design, engineering and history. Dean Herman advised the bachelors in the class not to get married. I didn't heed his advice and married Maureen and in a couple of years a daughter, Mauria, came into my world. Later a second daughter, Alixine, was born. To make ends meet I took on three jobs. One was at Van de Kamp's Bakery loading trucks on Thursday and Friday nights. Weekends I worked for an architect in White Center. My schedule at school gave me two long breaks on Tuesday and Thursday. I was able to land a part-time job drafting for the architectural firm of Jones, Lovegren, Helm and Jones. The exciting part of this job was working on Trader Vic restaurants. Lloyd Lovegren was a good friend of the Trader. His office designed every Trader Vic restaurant. One of the restaurants I made layouts of was going to be constructed in a space at the Idlewild Airport in New York, later renamed Kennedy International. The Trader was a character who liked to emphasize viewpoints with cuss words, which he frequently used no matter who was present.

Mr. Helms was the office manager. He worked behind a screen and occasionally popped out to make sure all pencils were busy. If there was too much conversation his head popped out from behind the screen like a Jack-in-the-box. We had two ten-minute breaks, one in the morning and one in the afternoon. Helms kept track of the time to the minute. In exactly 10 minutes he popped out from behind the screen to sharpen his pencil in a sharpener that hung on the wall in view of everyone. This was the signal to get back to work.

One of the draftsmen liked to play tricks on Helms, one of which was to put a stub of a pencil about 1½" long into the opening of the sharpener so helms couldn't get his pencil in the hole. We all watched with great amusement as Helms mumbled and fumbled taking the sharpener apart to clean it.

At school it was all work, but we managed to have fun too. We had an absent-minded professor, Lance Gowan, who would suddenly stop in the middle of a lecture and start reciting a grocery list. He was a fastidious dresser, with neatly combed graying hair on top of a very kindly face. He smiled a lot as he spoke. He wore glasses and always carried a pipe stuffed with tobacco. In the design class the professor walked amongst the students to critique the work as it progressed. Professor Gowan stopped at a desk and laid his pipe down while he talked to the student. He left, forgetting his pipe. The student said nothing. The following week the professor came through again, stopped and talked to the student. When finished, he picked up his pipe, lit it and went on the next student as if he had just laid it down.

The best story of all was when Prof. Gowan was taking his family to the movies. They all got into the car and he said he had to stop at his office to pick up something. He got out of the car, went into the office, did what he had to, went out the back door, got on the bus and went home, leaving his family sitting in the car.

Most of the students in the class were veterans of the Korean War. There was a sprinkling of high school grads. The older guys were all very serious about their studies. Another professor happened to comment that our class lacked the exuberance and chicanery of youth—a big mistake! He had just purchased a shiny new VW Beetle. While he was lecturing a bunch of students picked his car up and hauled it up the large flight of stairs and left it in the foyer of the architecture hall.

On another occasion the same professor was walking below the balcony of the 2nd floor. He was hit with paper bags filled with water. There were other pranks pulled and there was no more talk of youthful exuberance.

I had to make up math and science deficiencies that I did not fulfill in high school. I ended up taking physics from Prof. Nedermeyer whom I was told, was a co-winner of the Nobel Prize in some kind of atomic research. He lectured in the main auditorium where students listened intently, after which the group was broken up into classes of 15-20 students. I happened to get Nedermeyer as a class teacher.

Professor Nedermeyer was a thin man with wild flashing eyes and curly bushy hair that stood out in every direction. He acted as though he had a finger in a light socket at all times. He moved about nervously as he spoke. One day we had a problem that no one could figure out. A student asked the professor to show us how to get the answer. He started at one end of the blackboard in front of the class, working furiously with the chalk and mumbling incoherent phrases as he went. He covered the entire front board with mathematical hieroglyphics. Then he went to the board in the back of the room and we all turned our heads to watch. He continued almost covering the entire board and exclaimed with great exuberance, "Here is the answer!"

In the physics book the answers are all in the back of the book but the process to get the answer is what had to be worked out. He asked, "What's the answer in the book?" A student looked it up and it did not correspond with his numbers. He frantically looked at all his work and then wildly at the class and asked, "Did anyone see my mistake?" The sad part is we could not even follow what he had been scratching on the board.

The five years went by quickly. Our architectural basic design class started out with about 85 students. Out of that original group we graduated 14.

Neighbors

While attending school I had purchased a piece of property in White Center on 19th Avenue S.W. that had a small building on it. I remodeled it into a livable home. The property was purchased from Ma Ritchie, the lady who at one time owned the Glendale Tavern. There was no down payment and monthly payments were $25. It fit my budget nicely along with my GI Bill and part time jobs. My wife Maureen was working at Boeing. With our combined income we were able to make it. Each month I would drive to Ma Ritchie's house to give her the $25. She always invited me in for tea or coffee and tell me stories about her bartending days at the Glendale Tavern in White Center. I now wish I had been able to tape all of our conversations. She was a very large woman and could physically throw drunks out of the tavern, that is if Tommie Tucker, the policeman, was not around to do the job. Ma Ritchie had sold the tavern and constructed a restaurant in Burien called The Blue Ox. Later it became Jim Moore's Steak House.

The neighbors in White Center living on 19th Avenue were a tight-knit group and would keep an eye on each other's homes. Curly Witherbee, the district legislator, lived across the alley. Next door there was a Mr. Dunn who was a retired stonemason from England who helped me with the foundations of the house. He was forced into retirement early when a horse drawn carriage ran over him and ruined one of his legs. He always greeted me with a friendly smile. His accident left him with a very serious limp and he had to use a cane. He was not very tall and his limp and bow legs made him even shorter. He had a very round jovial face and blue eyes that twinkled. He spoke with a slight Cockney accent. His entire yard was made up of various creations of masonry— walls, walks and floral containers. Because of his bad leg he always worked sitting down even when setting bricks or mixing mortar.

Across the street were Rick and Patti with whom we socialized. Rick would help me with my car when I had problems. He was about 5'9", small and wiry with a head of curly brown hair. Behind horned-rimmed glasses were piercing brown eyes. He liked to drink and worked the graveyard shift at a cardboard plant maintaining machinery. Rick and Patti did not get along so well.

One day while mowing the lawn I heard shouts from their house. I shut the mower down so I could hear what Patti was yelling about. She was hysterical and incoherent. When I started to walk toward her, she gestured wildly to come quickly. She was shouting something about a gun cabinet. Rick was a hunter and had several rifles, shotguns and pistols locked in a gun cabinet that had glass panel doors. Rick had fallen through the gun cabinet and had severely cut the underside of his forearm, severed big arteries and the blood was squirting all over the living room.

I learned later the real story that led up to this tragic event. Rick working nights left Patti alone in the evenings. Evidently Patti and Rick's sister Emily were visiting taverns while Rick was at work. At a tavern with live music Patti had taken up with one of the musicians and was having an affair. Rick found out about it and drunk himself into a stupor. He raved like a lunatic and was threatening bodily harm. Patti had called Rick's sister and her boyfriend who was a policeman named William. He was a big man, about 6'4" and 250 pounds. They tried to get Rick to settle down but in a sudden burst of rage he jumped for the gun cabinet, obviously to get a gun, smashed the glass with his forearm and cut himself. Several pieces of glass stuck in his arm.

William was trying to hold Rick who now had an adrenalin surge making him very difficult to control. We had to get a tourniquet on his arm to stop the bleeding. I whipped off my belt and after a struggle was able to get it around his bicep and put several twists into it. Patti and Emily ran to start the car. William and I were finally able to get Rick into the back seat where William held him and I had his arm with the tourniquet. We sped off to the hospital, which was on the second floor of a building in West Seattle about 6 miles distant. Patti had called Rick's doctor who said he would be waiting for us.

In the car the tourniquet was not working well. Blood was still squirting out all over the place. William said, "Apply pressure directly." I clamped my hands over the wounds and squeezed tightly. This seemed to help but the blood was oozing out between my fingers. William said, "Hang a white cloth out the window," which was a signal of emergency and he said, "break the speed limit, maybe we can attract a police car along the way!" We sped from White Center to the West Seattle Junction leaning on the horn, yet did not encounter one police car the entire way.

By now I was soaked with Rick's blood. My shirt, pants and shoes were covered. It had clotted up in big blobs on my shoelaces so I could not even see them. We were instructed to come in the back way and use the freight elevator so as not to disrupt the people in the lobby. The freight elevator had a strange sequence of operation that no one seemed to understand. It would start up, go a few feet and stop. Through the wire mesh the doctor was yelling instructions as to how to operate it and we were yelling up that we couldn't make it work. It was a chaotic scene, blood everywhere, people yelling and Rick's sister said she was going to faint. William grabbed her and held on as I held Rick.

Finally we got the elevator to work and Rick was rushed into Emergency and immediately sedated. The doctor removed the glass and stitched him up. I was wandering around in the hall covered with blood and nurses came running up asking where I was cut. I explained what had happened and they told me to get out of sight as I might frighten other patients. After what seemed hours, the doctor came out and told us that Rick was all right and we could take him home. He was still somewhat sedated so it was a quiet ride home.

It was not long after this incident that Rick and Patti divorced. Rick was given custody of the children. Things quieted down for a while on 19th Avenue. Soon after the divorce he realized he needed help to raise the kids and he eventually met another lady—her name was Jenny.

Jenny was a pleasant lady with a pretty face and being large boned gave her the appearance of being heavy. She was easy to get along with and loved Rick's kids, as she had none of her own. It appeared that things might work out for him, but it wasn't long before Rick's drinking got him into trouble with Jenny. I was sorry to see them break up.

Soon after Jenny left, Rick was looking for a new wife. He had kids to care for. Soon he introduced us to another Jenny whom we named Jenny No. 2. She had a happy-go-lucky personality, dark hair and dark complexion, her face full and olive shaped. Her nose and features made her appear to be Native American. She was very stoutly built and looked like she could handle Rick if he got out of hand. Jenny liked to party and tip a few. She and Rick got along well together and it wasn't long before they were asking my wife and me to join them on a trip to the San Juan Islands. We talked it over and thought that Rick had his drinking under control and we could make a go of it. I had recently finished my first job in architecture and was having a tough time making ends meet. So this was a welcome vacation opportunity.

We headed north on a blustery day in August, with the dinghy I had built in tow. We decided to visit an uncle of Jenny's, who lived on the south tip of Camano Island. I don't know how much Rick had to drink before we weighed anchor but he was in a boisterous mood. Running his 26-foot Sabercraft wide open made the boat pound heavily on top of the waves. There was a slight drizzle falling and the south wind gave us a following sea. Rick was not paying much attention to his navigation and didn't see the giant log that was just behind a furl in a wave. It must have been at least 50 feet long and 2 feet in diameter.

It was fortunate that the boat hit the log in a T-bone fashion and went right over the top. The 100 h.p. Mercury motor flipped up and automatically shut down. The boat hit so hard it drove the ceiling light fixtures out of their recessed containers smashing them on the deck and galley table. It split the bottom of the dinghy that we were towing—the little boat I had so lovingly built was now useless. We quickly pulled up deck boards to see if we were taking on water. Miraculously, the boat held together.

Before all this happened Jenny had gone to the head to relieve herself. It must have been at least five minutes before she came out screaming a stream of obscenities that would make the devil blush. I guess whatever was in the toilet bowl was thrust upward by the force of the blow and it took her some time to get cleaned up. This incident sobered everyone quickly. We were able to get the motor started and made our way at top speed toward shore. After thoroughly checking below decks we determined there was no serious hull damage so we continued at a moderate pace with a watchful eye.

We found Uncle Jack's place on Camano Island and he hailed us ashore. Uncle Jack was a hermit, living with his pet rooster named Euripides. He had a grizzly appearance behind an unkempt white beard, wearing a floppy hat and bib overalls with one strap hanging down. He was an intelligent, well-read man who loved to quote Shakespeare and poetry. He invited us in to his cabin and poured us a drink. He sat down in his rocking chair and Euripides hopped up and sat on his shoulder. Evening approached and Uncle Jack held us in awe, quoting poetry and Shakespeare. In the dim light of evening you could see many books on shelves about the living room. I do not recall seeing a television set. He did have a phonograph and we listened to classical music. The whole place had the feeling of putting on an old shoe that after many years had comfortably taken the shape of your foot. The wind was blowing hard and the heat from the fireplace with the drinks mellowed all of us and we melted into the night.

The next morning we were up early to make the next leg of the journey.

The wind had died down. Uncle Jack fixed breakfast and with a wave of his hat bade us farewell with his rooster standing beside him.

We made it all the way into Roche Harbor without any serious mishaps. We found a place to tie up at one of the docks. Rick and I decided to check out the restaurant and bar located in the hotel. The girls wanted to take their time to change and clean up. We told them we would make reservations and meet them in the cocktail lounge. It was a very friendly place and the bartender was talkative. We sat at the bar and struck up a conversation with him.

He told us about the old lime quarry and what a neat place it was for swimming. He said that when he got off work around midnight he was going there for a dip and asked us to join him. We said we would think about it and talk to the girls. The lounge was busy and it kept the bartender on the move. Soon he appeared saying, "I mixed this drink and it was a mistake," then offered it to us in lieu of tossing it in the sink. "Sure, we'll take it!" We split it and enjoyed our freebee. Soon he was back again with another mistake. Rick and I looked at each other and said, "This is an all right place."

The next time he came by we ordered two "mistakes" that appeared promptly. It was getting late and still nothing of the wives. Rick went to investigate and found that they were having a party of their own and would arrive when they felt like it. We went back to our drinks and waited for them at the bar.

A gregarious fellow appeared and sat down next to us and struck up a conversation. He said he was from Seattle and had just arrived with his parents on their yacht. He said he was a graduate of Garfield High School as was Rick. Soon yarns were being exchanged about this teacher and that teacher. The strange thing about this guy is that he brought his own portable bar, set it up on the counter and was offering free

215

drinks. This did not go well with the bartender. The fellow obviously came from a wealthy family, revealing his status after he had loosened his tongue. The more he drank the louder he became and soon was being very obnoxious. The bartender mistakenly thought he was a friend of ours. The girls finally showed up and were a bit tipsy. It was too late for dinner and the bartender asked us to get our friend out. We told him we would do what we could. We talked him into packing up his bar and asked him to show us his boat. Rick on one side and I on the other propped him up and the five of us waddled off to the dock where the boat was moored.

It truly was a beautiful yacht, 60 feet long in the style of the old classic mosquito fleet that plied passengers throughout Puget Sound in the early 1900s. There was a lot of varnished wood and highly polished brass. We were shown the wheelhouse and staterooms. All of the interior was of mahogany, varnished to where you could see reflections. We asked about his parents and he said they were staying at the hotel nearby. At the mention of his parents he became very agitated and suddenly violent. We all disembarked and were standing on the dock. It was past midnight. He started yelling and screaming obscenities and swinging his fists wildly. One of them caught Jenny in the eye and down she went, fortunately not into the water. Her purse went overboard and sank. I jumped on him and had him on his back and punched him several times. Finally Rick and I gathered him up and threw him back into his boat. There was a lot of commotion that aroused several boaters who came out and yelled for us to shut up and go to bed. We went back to the bar and reported everything to the bartender who said he would call the sheriff in the morning.

Our small boat did not have bathing facilities. Roche Harbor had an outbuilding where you could shower, shave and clean up. Early the next morning Rick and I were using the shower and we overheard talk about the big fight on the dock last night. We looked at each other and smiled. The sheriff came and took a picture of Jenny's black eye and took down our statements. We all went out on the dock to talk to the perpetrator and found that the boat had gone—the family had boarded their grand yacht in the night and left. The sheriff was able to get some divers to go down into the water and retrieve Jenny's purse and other belongings from the bottom of the harbor.

The next evening we went to the hotel bar and the bartender loaded us up with more "mistakes" hoping we would all join him for a swim in the quarry. He showed us a bottle that he had filled up with mixed drinks and was looking forward to a party. We all drank too much and I staggered out after closing, heading to the lime quarry. We passed a lighted swimming pool and decided to jump in there instead. The pool was locked up so we climbed over the fence. The men stripped to their shorts and the girls to their panties and bras and we all hopped in making a lot of noise. We were quickly discovered and promptly thrown out by the caretaker. This ended our San Juan vacation and we headed home to White Center.

Peeping Toms

White Center was not without exciting nights. One evening Mr. Witherbee came running over to our house to tell us there was a Peeping Tom in the neighborhood. We quickly alerted our neighbors. A posse was formed and quietly moved out down the alley to try to catch the villain. We saw him atop a garbage can peeping in another neighbor's window. As we approached he spotted us and jumped off the can with a clatter rousing another neighbor. We chased him but could not catch him. We notified other neighbors and put out a Peeping Tom alert.

One evening our friends Rick and Patti across the street went out on the town. They had hired a babysitter to watch the kids. The babysitter put the kids to bed and had called her boyfriend. I happened to look out of my front window across to Rick's house. The bedroom faced the street. The white shade was pulled but the bright lights in the bedroom were on. I have never witnessed such a sexual silhouette show in my life. They were unaware that their movements shown brightly through the white shades. A few days later I told Rick about it and he said that the show they saw was lousy and they should have stayed home.

Working as an Architect

I went to work for an architect in Auburn where I ran into a classmate named Archie Fry. After working there for a while we decided to open up our own office in Burien. We teamed up with another architect, Dick Bissel, and rented a little office building in Seahurst. Dick was a registered architect in Washington State. Archie and I did not have an architect's license as yet so we called ourselves Allied Architects and Designers. It was not long before Archie decided to return to Auburn where he knew more potential clients. Dick and I stuck it out in Seahurst. I joined a number of local clubs including the Burien White Center Rotary club to establish connections with the business community.

Near Cremation

Dick Yarington, who owned a funeral home in White Center, belonged to the Burien White Center Rotary Club. Discovering I was an architect, he asked me to visit his home as he wanted to remodel. I drew plans for him and later he had me do a number of minor remodels to the funeral home. One day he called and asked me to redo his crematorium. I told him I was not familiar with crematoriums and he should look for someone experienced in that field. He said, "Don't worry, I have a book that shows all the details, you just have to measure the space and show the location of the new furnace." I was reluctant, but he said, "Come over, I'll buy lunch and we'll talk about it."

I did not like the idea of drawing plans for a crematorium, but Dick had given me quite a bit of work so I reluctantly agreed. As I was measuring the existing crematory I remarked, "Dick, this furnace is still hot." He said, "Oh yes, we just finished a cremation," and as he spoke opened the oven door, reached in and said, "See, here is part of the skull." He scrunched it in his hand and threw the ash back in through the open door.

I finished my work as quickly as possible and went back to the office to make the drawings. Dick was planning to take the old crematory out, which was oil-fired and replace it with a gas-fired unit. He said the oil-fired unit took eight hours to dispose of the remains and the gas-fired unit would do it in less than four hours. Dick said people complained about the black smoke coming from the chimney and that the oil burner was not efficient. The new gas unit would have a 1,500,000 BTU front burner and a 1,000,000 after burner to eliminate all traces of smoke.

Two months later Dick called up, asked me to come over, as he wanted to show me something. I said, "Dick, if you are cooking something in your new furnace, I don't want to see it." He insisted, "Come over and I'll buy lunch." Again I went with some trepidation. We met in his office and he immediately took me to the new crematory. He just wanted to show how it fired up.

On the wall was a control panel that looked like it came out of an airplane. Lights were flashing as his assistant started pushing all kinds of buttons. Dick and I were standing in front of the oven door looking straight into the furnace. There was a giant roar as the burners came on. Suddenly we were both enveloped in a ball of fire. His assistant had forgotten to push the button to feed oxygen into the furnace. The flame jumped out of the furnace to grab the oxygen in the room. I had a full beard and mustache at the time that was nicely singed. Still shaking, Dick said, "Let's get out of here and have some lunch."

Seahurst

The office building we rented was owned by Mr. Carleton. He was from Mississippi and spoke with a deep southern accent. He was about 5'6" with a slight frame and a crop of white hair beneath a worn-out Fedora. He wore glasses and always had a ready smile. He had a mint condition Model A Ford that he drove to Burien and the post office. When in his car he always wore driving gloves which were a pair of white garden gloves. You could see the gloves a half block away affixed to the top of the steering wheel. He moved into this area long before Ambaum Boulevard was a paved road. He related how when he drove to White Center he crossed through Salmon Creek that cut across the graveled road, and when the salmon were spawning how he used to dodge them as they struggled across the road.

Years before, our little office in Carleton's building had been Gunther's Real Estate office. At that time there were very few roads and the streetcar line ended in Seahurst. Many people came out for the day, prepared with picnic baskets, to look at the land around Lake

Burien and Gregory Heights that Mr. Gunther had subdivided. He created a viewing tower from a huge topped fir tree around which was constructed a circular stairway. Mr. Gunther would take people to the top of the tower and point out the approximate location of the lot they were buying. The stump of that tower/tree still remains at the corner of 22nd Avenue and 152nd Street.

Over the years, practicing as an architect, I have had many interesting clients and projects. I soon learned I had to play the role of a psychologist. I was amazed at the couples who try to revive their relationships through the design and construction of a new residence. Entering as the third party, I found that the architect could easily become the sounding board for their arguments. Sadly, the new house did not always provided the sought-after fix for the clients. Not infrequently, after they had moved in, a divorce followed.

On one particular occasion everything ended happily, although the design process went on for over a year. A doctor and his wife came to see me about designing a house. The doctor did all the talking and said he was interested in Japanese-styled architecture. I told him I had spent a couple of years in Japan so we immediately hit it off. I prepared preliminary studies for them and after a time they were all rejected. More studies were prepared and again rejected.

One day they both came into the office and we were discussing the latest drawings. The wife, who had been silent through most of the meetings, suddenly blurted out, "OK, you buy the lot next door and build the house I want and you can do whatever you want on your lot." It turned out that she wanted an Early American-styled house like some of her friends had. None of this had come out previously. Eventually the doctor prevailed and the Japanese-styled house was constructed. After they moved in she was thrilled with the outcome. She confided in me that what she really wanted was something "different" but didn't know exactly what. For years afterward she used to call and thank me for the design of the house.

Another project that I designed for a young couple turned out nicely but ended in divorce. The young lady was vivacious, attractive and flirtatious. She called me many times to have lunch on the pretense of discussing the house design. She would call me at home nightly, which didn't sit well with my wife. One evening she called to discuss plumbing fixtures. As I spoke with her I could hear water splashing about. I asked, "Are you washing dishes?" "No I am in the tub taking a bath." She had a low sexy voice like Marlene Dietrich. Eventually the plans came to fruition and in the summer the house was under construction. On warm sunny days she would show up at the construction site wearing a very brief bikini—there was nothing left to the imagination. The contractor took notice of this. To make a long story short, she left her husband and kids and took off with the contractor who likewise left his wife and kids.

I was told by a friend to call a lady named Anna Avery. She owned the Seven Seas Tavern on First Avenue in downtown Seattle. She wanted to remodel the tavern and the front of her building. The Maritime Union was next door and above the tavern were rental rooms. I made an appointment to meet her at the tavern. It was a sight to behold—the roughest looking bunch of people you'd ever want to see were sitting at the bar, some with large boils on the backs of their necks. Sailors and merchant seamen waiting for a call to get on a ship were sitting around guzzling beer.

The Seven Seas Tavern at 1966 First Avenue in Seattle)

A lady with frizzy blond hair and glasses was tending bar. I asked, "Anna?" She said, "No," and pointed to a door behind me that was under a stair that led to the upstairs rooms. I was puzzled and knocked politely. No one answered and I knocked again, but still no answer. I told the lady at the bar that no one was there. "She's in there alright, knock hard, she can't hear too well." I pounded on the door and heard a voice, "Who is it?" I said, "It's the architect." She invited me in. There is not much room under a stair and in the dim light I saw she was counting her money. She was a tiny thing with a nicely coiffed head of white hair. She said, "We won't talk here," as she took off her shoe and then stuffed money into it. Then in a strong voice said, "We're going out to lunch." She said she always kept her money in her shoe because she was afraid someone in that part of town would knock her down and snatch her purse. Anna grabbed me by the arm, pulled me up close and said, "Let's go."

223

Everyone at the bar knew Anna and waved goodbye. At the door going out we ran into her husband, a short, very stout man with glasses so thick they magnified the size of his eyes. It made his eyeballs look so large that I stared impolitely. He asked, "Where are you going?" Anna answered quickly, "This is my architect. We're going to lunch to discuss the remodel of this building." He made a feeble protest but Anna, who still had my arm, pulled me out through the door. On the street, I believe everyone we ran into knew Anna including the two burly policemen walking their beat. All wished her a good day. We found a restaurant and she told me all the things that she wanted done to the building. She also said that her husband was opposed to the project. It was his opinion that a facelift would not bring in any more money. But Anna was tired of the worn out look of the place and after lunch she gave me a tour of the building.

Back at the Seven Seas Tavern she told me what she wanted done to the exterior, adding "Never mind the Union Hall entrance." Anna gave me a tour of the interior including the men's restroom. It was the first time I had encountered what she called a vomitory. A tiled space with a grab bar about shoulder height where one could hang on and relieve himself before going back for more beer. The structure must have dated back to the days of the Barbary Coast. She opened a door showing me a chute that went to the alley below. Sailors used to be Shanghaied and shoved into the chute to a waiting cart below. Indeed the place needed a great deal of upgrading and modernization. I was impressed by the strong-willed little lady and her determination to do something with her place. Today sadly, my work and the entire building has been torn down and replaced.

Another client was a retired army general, Jeff Beeman. He and his sister owned property on Lummi Island. When he found out that I had served in the army under General MacArthur, he decided that I was an all right guy. When I told him that I just held the rank of staff sergeant, he quickly said, "Do not berate your grade, it was the sergeants that ran the army." This pat on the back made me feel good. Earlier I had talked about Lummi Island and the Indian reef netters who had built shacks on the property now owned by the general. They had remained vacant for years.

In the 1960s the hippie movement was in full swing. The hippies invaded the island and set up housekeeping in theses structures. The general was having difficulty trying to evict them. He was threatened physically. The general devised a plan of attack. He, like General Custer, would confront the hippies directly. His plan was to get them all to come out and talk to him in the center of a clearing. In the meantime, friends that he had organized would sneak through the woods and shower the shacks with gasoline while the general was arguing with the group. Matches were tossed and a giant conflagration erupted. The hippies took off in all directions never to be seen again. The general liked this story and each time it was told it got better. I remodeled the house that he had on the property and later designed a home for his sister on an adjoining parcel.

I designed a medical facility for a doctor who was known to be a notorious philanderer. He told me that he had a route that he followed on a carefully memorized schedule. Coming home late at night after one of his escapades he became aware of a horrible irritation in his crotch and around his genitals. He quickly found a flashlight and locked himself in the bathroom. Upon close inspection he observed a swarm of creepy crawlers known as crabs. What to do?

His wife was asleep in the next room and he worried that he might infect her. Pulling his pants up he went into the garage where there was of collection of garden pesticides. Selecting a can of Black Flag, he read the label—kills flying insects at 40 feet. Well, he thought, at six inches this should wipe them out. A few moments after spraying he realized what he had done. The highly toxic chemical created a volcanic inflammation of the tender skin. Not being able to scream from the pain, he bit his tongue and ran back into the house and jumped in the shower. After an hour of scrubbing with soap and water the pain was tolerable. Drying himself he then crawled into bed next to his wife. His last thoughts were, what if I had caught them from her? (The epitome of passing the buck!)

An interesting project that I was involved with was a small deli restaurant located in the lower floors of the Trans-America Building in San Francisco. The design was done by Gull Design, which hired me to do the working drawings. The walls were huge porcelain panels with pictures of San Francisco from the late 1800s. The setting was a street corner and if you looked around the room, it was as if you were standing at that intersection viewing the surrounding buildings. The floor replicated the cobblestone street. Lampposts were cast to look exactly like the lampposts of that period. It was very well done to the last detail. I had the opportunity to visit the place after it was finished and it definitely felt as if it were the year 1860. I do not know if the place still exists.

In White Center I became acquainted with John Roby, a colorful local character. Looking at him you wouldn't think he had a dime. He said he made his money trading and selling goods in various countries of South East Asia. With a motorized canoe he plied various rivers in Thailand and Malaysia. He developed a great deal of property in White Center. He was short of stature and overweight with a paunchy belly. His clothes hung loosely over his body. He wore a baseball cap. His face was jowly and he was always in good spirits. In his pick-up truck a parrot would ride along sitting on his shoulder. He had a can of peanuts by his side that he fed to the parrot and would occasionally pop some into his own mouth and also offer them to me.

He would tell me he had so much money he didn't know what to do with it. I would jokingly say, "Adopt me and I will help you figure that out." I drew plans for a building to be constructed in White Center. He did not like the idea of getting a building permit and thought it took too long. While the permit was being processed he started his excavation. There was a great deal of earth required to be removed from this site. This left a 16 foot vertical cut at the rear of the property. The job was red-tagged after a neighbor complained. This made it extremely difficult to process the permit as they looked upon this as a project where someone doesn't play by the rules. After a great deal of haggling he eventually got the permit and completed the building. Years later my brother bought this building after he had enough of teaching.

A chicken farmer named Lassiter living in White Center called me and wanted to remodel his house. He was a wiry looking man about 5'8" tall. He wore striped bib overalls that covered a red shirt. He had a very ruddy complexion with bright blue eyes. He wore a woven hat. The life had gone out of the straw so the brim went up and down around his head. He raised thousands of chickens in coops north of his house. They were butchered, packaged and sold to grocery chains. He spoke with a faint Southern accent. He told me he was from the Midwest— Kansas I believe—where he used to be a bank robber. He was caught and served his time. He met a lady and they moved west to start a new life. She was a very pleasant friendly woman who loved to cook chicken. At every meeting I had with them I was served a meal of fried chicken that I thoroughly enjoyed. Mr. Lassiter said that it was his wife who straightened him out. He also told me that for years, every time there was a bank robbery in the area he was interviewed by the FBI. He was proud to tell them that he was just a hard-working chicken farmer. When I left I was always given several packages of fresh chicken parts.

One day I received a long-distance call from Ellensburg, Washington. It was Harold, my old boss that I had worked for as a steeplejack. He had retired from his business and purchased a motel in town and wanted to add a substantial number of units. I drove across the Cascade Mountains to discuss the addition. He was still the same Harold I had known years ago, still vibrant and full of enthusiasm. He told me business was so good he had to expand. He was located across the street from the Court House. He said there were so many customers at noon, who he called hot-sheeters, that he had to add units. He explained to me that hot-sheeters were in and out in about one hour and because they didn't even get under the covers, he didn't have to change the sheets. I drew plans for an additional wing and a couple of years later a larger addition. As the real estate people put it—location, location, location.

My practice in architecture has put me in touch with people in all walks of life. Each client is another story. The smaller projects were always agreed upon with a handshake, the more complicated ones with a letter of agreement. The very large ones were done with a formal American Institute of Architects printed contract. I can recall only two or three handshake agreements that went bad. After 45 years of business I thought this an OK record.

I do not know where the term "Rat City" originated. What I do know is that rats exist the world over. I have never seen an overabundance of the creatures in White Center. The area has always been in a continual state of flux. Many buildings have been neglected and have fallen into a state of disrepair and exhibit a ratty appearance. Maybe this is a moniker generated by that outlook. There was a cartoon printed on a shirt that depicted a rat scratching his head asking for directions to White Center.

"Where's White Center?")

Growing up in such a diversified community has taught me to deal with people in various positions of wealth and stature. Today the White Center community is even more diverse. You can find people from S.E. Asia, India, China, Samoa, Latinos, African-Americans, Russians and probably others I am not aware of. The needs of these various ethnic groups become apparent in the shops and grocery stores serving them. This diversity gives this area a character that is unique. Many of the structures that I had worked on have been swept up in this new wave of activity. The area that I had known as a youth is gone. It has left me with many memories. After all, as the Russian adage has it, *Zhizn dvizheniye*— "Life is movement."

At this writing I continue working as an architect. So my story continues and as more memories become memorable moments I can finish this story.

Printed in the United States
154648LV00010B/104/P

9 781434 389039